W9-CSF-976

snakes as pets

fourth edition

by DR. HOBART M. SMITH

Cover:
Chionactis palarostris palarostris. Photo by Richard L. Holland.

Frontispiece: A Blacknecked Gartersnake, *Thamnophis cyrtopsis cyrtopsis*, nestled in greenery. The large dark paired nape spots are especially diagnostic. Photo by G. Marcuse.

ISBN 0-87666-908-9

Distributed in the U.S.A. by T.F.H. Publications, Inc., 211 West Sylvania Avenue, P.O. Box 27, Neptune City, N.J. 07753; in England by T.F.H. (Gt. Britain) Ltd., 13 Nutley Lane, Reigate, Surrey; in Canada to the book store and library trade by Clarke, Irwin & Company, Clarwin House, 791 St. Clair Avenue West, Toronto 10, Ontario; in Canada to the pet trade by Rolf C. Hagen Ltd., 3225 Sartelon Street, Montreal 382, Quebec; in Southeast Asia by Y.W. Ong, 9 Lorong 36 Geylang, Singapore 14; in Australia and the south Pacific by Pet Imports Pty. Ltd., P.O. Box 149, Brookvale 2100, N.S.W., Australia. Published by T.F.H. Publications, Inc. Ltd., The British Crown Colony of Hong Kong.

Contents

ACKNOWLEDGMENTS

Many friends and associates have contributed importantly to the preparation of this book. Mr. Frank Dittrich has been the benevolent consultant, adviser and exhorter throughout. The illustrations I owe to the courtesy of the late Dr. Norman Hartweg, Dr. L.M. Klauber, Dr. P.W. Smith and others. For factual information I am indebted to Miss Roberta Froom, Dr. S.C. Kendeigh, Mrs. Norma Rothman, Dr. William Stickel and to many other friends and correspondents. Most drawings are by Dr. Charles A. McLaughlin, now Director of Education of the San Diego Zoo.

ILLUSTRATIONS

American Museum of Natural History: 11, bottom; 111; 140; 143, bottom.
Boys and Smith: 15
Brown, Robert Louis: 36, bottom; 48, top; 97; 113, top.
del Toro, Dr. Miguel Alvarez: 116
Dodd, F., Jr.: 33, bottom; 61, bottom; 64, top; 104; 112, bottom; 117, bottom; 120.
Gannon, Robert: 102, bottom.
Holland, Richard L.: 18, 30, 32, 37, top; 40; 41; 44; 45; 49, bottom; 52, bottom; 56; 60; 64, bottom; 100, top; 101, top; 109; 110; 113, bottom; 121; 124; 125; 128, top; 131; 135; 136, bottom; 137, top; 139; 142, bottom; 145; 146.
Illinois Natural History Survey: 31
Imgrund, Paul: 67, top; 102, top.
Klauber, L.M.: 144
Knaack, Dr. Karl: 112, top.
Langhammer, James K.: 36, top; 37, bottom; 48, bottom; 49, top; 52, top; 57; 101, bottom; 105; 108.
Lovrity, Joseph: 68
Marcuse, Gerhard: 12; 17, top; 61, top; 86; 117, top.
New York Zoological Society: 115, 119.
Pope, Clifford: 82, bottom; 83, bottom; 122; 130; 138; 142, top.
Roberts, Mervin F.: 77; 106.
Smith, Dr. H.M.: 33, top; 53, bottom; 128, bottom
Smith, Dr. P.W.: 141, bottom.
University of Florida Press (from *Guide to the Reptiles, Amphibians, and Freshwater Fishes of Florida*): 82, top; 83, top; 123; 141, top.
University of Michigan Museums (from Ortenburger): 143, top.

1. Snakes as Pets

Snakes are the world's most exciting safe pets. If you don't think so, just gauge the reaction of the average person when confronted by a snake, even a captive snake. And if you think snakes are not safe—well, they are just like your fellow men: some are as dangerous as maniacs, but most of them are as safe as your next-door neighbors. Of course, you have to know how to choose your company—and your pets.

In this book we shall introduce a few of the snakes which make safe home pets, tell you how to keep them and review some interesting facts about them. If you find snakes fascinating, as they are to many people, let us warn you **never to experiment** with snakes of unknown species. Many entirely innocent-looking snakes are really harmful. The snake you find in some backyard may be a good pet—or it may be a considerable risk. If you buy your snakes, be sure to get them from a reliable dealer exactly as you specify, or assure yourself otherwise that the snakes are safe, before you handle them.

Why Snakes?

Many parents, although basically tolerant of the activities of their offspring, feel like martyrs when confronted by a request for a pet snake or by the accomplished fact of a snake in hand. The truth is that the martyrdom is amply rewarded in the benefits that can befall the owner of the pet. There is a sense of accomplishment in successfully maintaining a completely dependent animal; in becoming intimately familiar with something that commonly and unjustifiably is abhorred; in exploring a completely new relationship; and in expressing individuality without risk of overwhelming condemnation.

Probably the most common initial reason for selecting a snake as a pet is the fact that it is odd, different. One quickly learns, however, that oddity is the least of the attractiveness of snakes as pets. They are quiet, unobtrusive, do not demand frequent attention, are relatively hardy, do not transport diseases that can affect humans, are clean, odorless and need little special equipment for their care.

In many ways they are ideal pets, but there are certain limitations. Provision of food requires some ingenuity (see section of **Feeding**, page 50), and the responsiveness of snakes leaves something to be desired in the eyes of many. Although snakes actually are more responsive than they are commonly thought to be, the fact remains that at best they will never heel like a dog, sing like a canary or purr like a cat. Each person must decide for himself whether these or other attributes outweigh the satisfaction of keeping snakes as pets. In weighing pros and cons, do not underestimate the responsiveness of snakes. Think what *they* can do for *you*, as well as what you must do for them.

No one can fail to gain knowledge and understanding of the meaning of life by becoming familiar with the ways of so handicapped an animal as a snake. It can be of great psychological benefit in many ways. Young and old, sick and healthy, outcast and comrade, scholar and illiterate alike can appreciate the mental lift that possession and care of snakes can provide.

"I'll never forget the day that my youngest son received a small snake," a father once wrote me. "I won't say that he was a timid boy, but I'll tell you one thing:

when he took that snake out of his pocket in a group he was the star of the room. He was shining and bright as a new penny; it really did something for him." And in a Midwest reformatory a snake kept by one of the instructors is one of the most valuable means of evoking response from withdrawn, antagonistic boys. Any child can understand that snakes are essentially helpless except for the ability of some to bite. Many do not have even that recourse, and all are effectively deaf, have no limbs with which to flee or to protect themselves, and must take care of all their needs by movements of the body and the head. Imagine any four-limbed animal surviving on its own without benefit of hands or feet! Snakes are nature's most spectacular success story under seemingly insurmountable odds—and children often seem intuitively more sensitive to this fact than their elders. Small wonder that they may identify with snakes or at least feel highly sympathetic to them!

The Risks of Snakes as Pets

Not knowing just exactly what makes snakes dangerous, uninformed people often fear the tongue and the tail. Neither can actually inflict any harm in any species. The tongue is an accessory device for smelling, catching airborne odorous particles and conveying them to a special olfactory organ. It is a soft structure much like our own, except in shape. The tail likewise is harmless, having no venomous properties whatsoever. The reports of a tail stinger in snakes are wholly fictitious. Biting is the only way in which a native United States snake can do actual physical damage to adult humans.

All species have teeth, most have an ample supply in four rows in the upper jaws and two rows in the lower. Deadly venomous species have an enlarged pair of these teeth at the front of the upper jaws, one tooth on each side. These enlarged teeth—fangs—conduct venom into the bitten parts (see Figs. 1, 2). Common pet species, of course, lack fangs and venom (see Fig. 3).

ALL snakes can bite. Pet species are reluctant to bite, some absolutely refusing to bite unless the mouth is forced open. Should you be bitten by a non-venomous species, your only concern need be for a secondary infection caused by foreign organisms introduced into the scratches. The only treatment needed is a prompt painting of the scratches with iodine or other disinfectant.

The bite of a large non-venomous snake can be rather painful, but it is not at all dangerous, except when caused by Boas, Pythons, and a few other very large forms. Any snake bite can be much less painful if one remembers, as the snake sinks in his teeth, not to jerk the bitten part. This reflex results in simply tearing the slender teeth through the flesh, causing a much more extensive laceration than would be caused by the bite alone.

Otherwise, the species of snakes discussed in the following pages as pets are wholly harmless creatures. Some species, especially Watersnakes and Gartersnakes, void excrement profusely, sometimes throwing it about by wildly lashing body and tail, but this reaction is, at the most, maintained for a few weeks only. After a short period in captivity, such defenses are seldom used.

A few other species, Ringneck snakes particularly, secrete a strong-smelling fluid from the paired scent glands at the base of the tail, emerging at the anus. Though all snakes have scent glands, only a few use them in the manner described. Watersnakes and Gartersnakes may combine the scent secretion with excrement into a doubly-offensive mixture. But all usually fail to secrete the scent fluid after a short time—even 24 hours—in captivity. It is ordinarily a response to extreme fright—a last resort.

Because snakes learn quickly that they are not in

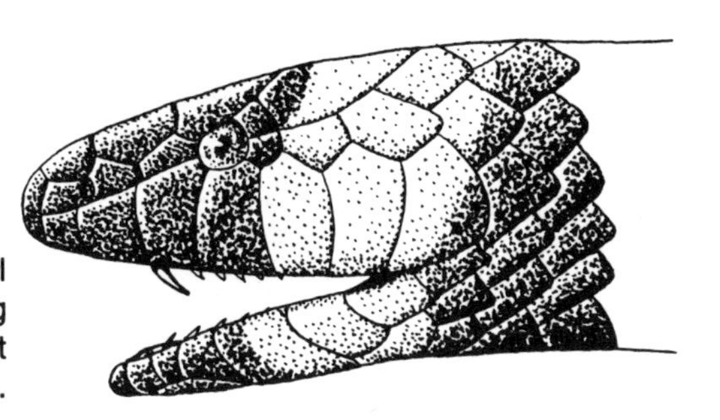

Figure 1. Coral snake, showing fixed front fangs.

Figure 2. Rattlesnake with movable front fangs in extended position for biting. In striking the mouth would be opened much wider, and the fangs would be more extended.

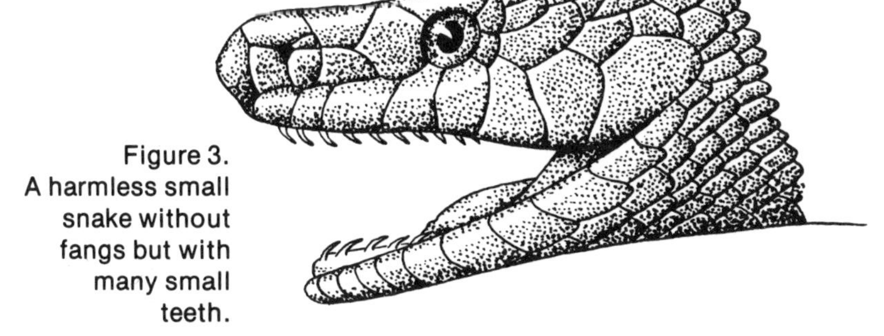

Figure 3. A harmless small snake without fangs but with many small teeth.

Figure 4. This Bullsnake is hissing in a defensive pose. Ordinarily a hissing snake has its lips only slightly parted, not open as wide as they are shown here.

mortal danger in captivity they soon cease to react violently to handling. Their adjustment to captivity continually improves and in the end they become docile animals that trust their captors implicitly. Although the speed of adjustment varies with different species, there is no snake which cannot be tamed with patient and proper care. Snakes which can be tamed with the least effort naturally make the best pets.

Snakes are often disliked because their skin is thought to be slimy. Anyone who has actually handled them knows this to be untrue. Most pet species have a smooth, glossy and clean skin. Snakes have fewer truly objectionable qualities than most mammals, or even birds.

When alarmed or provoked, many harmless snakes wiggle the end of the tail, and wiggling against a resonant object like dry leaves or the side of a wooden cage may produce an astonishing rattle-like sound.

Bullsnakes, Hognose snakes, and some others hiss rather loudly when alarmed or provoked. The Bullsnake especially produces a loud and often frightening sound (see Fig. 4). The hiss of the Hognose snake is a complete bluff, for the snake does not bite, even though it may lash out with its head (the mouth closed) at the intruder. Neither these nor any other U.S. snakes expel a venomous vapor, folklore notwithstanding.

Commonly snakes like the Hognose, which flatten or spread the body, especially in the neck region, are regarded as poisonous. The notion very likely originated in connection with the Spreading Cobra of the Old World, which certainly is deadly poisonous. But no such venomous snake with this behaviorism occurs in the United States. Hognose snakes are perhaps the world's most accomplished bluffers. They spread like a Cobra, yet are not venomous; they hiss and strike out with the

Figure 5. A young Hognose snake in the act of "spreading," an initial stage in its complex ritual of bluffing.

Figure 6. A closeup of an *Ophisaurus,* one of the legless lizards often mistaken for snakes. Note the eyelids and the slitlike ear opening behind the mouth. Neither occurs in true snakes.

head, yet do not bite; and they flop on their backs and play dead, yet remain keenly aware of their surroundings.

Value of Snakes

Snakes have been of importance to man in innumerable ways, none conspicuous, but in their sum of great magnitude. Direct benefits have been derived from use of the skins, a multi-million dollar enterprise every year; use as food, for the flesh is never poisonous, as is that of many fishes, some turtles, and even some mammals; and use of the venom in medicine. Many illnesses can be treated with venom, and the venom is used in preparing "antivenin" that counteracts snake poisoning, and in many experimental studies on venom action and its counteraction.

Indirect benefits accrue from the predation by snakes on noxious animals such as insects, rats, mice, gophers and even other snakes, and by their role in removal of weaklings and carcasses of dead animals. Even though sometimes snakes feed upon the eggs and young of desirable birds, their sum total effect upon man is beneficial. It has been calculated that every Bullsnake is worth $25 a year to farmers and to the national economy, as measured by the destruction that would be caused by rodents which the snake eats. Killing a Bullsnake has been likened to tearing up a handful of $5 bills.

Snakes are of great value as clues to the history of vertebrates, since they are related to the ancestors of man. They can, like ants, give many lessons of exemplary value to man. They also are an object lesson in the achievement of Nature in constructing a marvelously efficient animal despite anatomical shortcomings that in other similar lines of evolution have proved fatal. The adaptation of snakes to life despite their deficiencies is one of Nature's greatest achievements.

How to Distinguish Venomous Species from Non-Venomous Species

In this book only the kinds of snakes occuring in the United States are discussed. Foreign species are omitted chiefly because as a result of governmental restrictions on their importation, they are now only rarely obtainable. As a rule, they are obtainable only from dealers who can be relied on to specify whether a given species is non-venomous. All general information given here applies to foreign as well as to domestic species, but your dealer, local museum or school teacher should be consulted to supply specific information on the proper diet for exotic kinds.

Moreover, we do not discuss in this book the care of dangerously venomous species, since clearly they do not make suitable pets. Such snakes should be kept only by persons having a definite purpose and long experience. Most persons who venture to keep venomous snakes are sooner or later bitten. Intense suffering is invariably the result, and death follows occasionally. Since these animals are not suitable pets, they should not be forced into that role.

It should be understood that here and elsewhere in this book reference to "poisonous" or "venomous" snakes implies only the dangerous species. All so-called "non-poisonous" species have a saliva which can be irritating if it enters the flesh in exceptional quantities. It is rare indeed that enough does penetrate even with a chewing bite to cause any reaction, but it can and does happen. And in some snakes of this and other countries a few rear teeth are enlarged and, in some species, grooved so that the saliva can flow into a wound a little more rapidly than in snakes with smoothly tapering, equal-sized teeth. But even in these the saliva is non-toxic or only mildly toxic to humans, and the snakes are regarded as "mildly" venomous, at most. The species so modified fall into the following groups: Cateye snake, Coffeesnake, Flathead snakes, Groundsnakes, Hognose snakes, Hooknose snakes, Leafnose snakes, Lyresnake, Nightsnake, Sandsnake, Shovelnose snakes, Slender snake and Vinesnake. Most (20) of the 27 species of these groups would have much difficulty biting a person, and it would be virtually impossible for at least 13 of those 20.

The dangerously poisonous snakes of our area, of the Cobra family (family Elapidae) (the two genera and species of Coralsnakes and in Hawaii the Yellow-bellied Seasnake) and of the pit viper family (family Viperidae) (two species of moccasins of the genus *Agkistrodon*, two species of Pigmy Rattlesnakes of the genus *Sistrurus*, and 13 species of Mailed Rattlesnakes of the genus *Crotalus*) all have a saliva more toxic than any other snakes; more importantly, they have a pair of large, hollow front teeth that are directly connected with salivary gland ducts, so considerable quantities of the toxic saliva can be injected when the snake bites. In none of the other snakes is there a direct connection of salivary glands and the teeth. They are in much the same state as most other land vertebrates, such as dogs, cats, or even human beings, whose saliva is indeed somewhat toxic to a bitten person, but which usually has little effect because there is no mechanism for introducing very much of the saliva, and what is introduced is commonly washed out with water or flowing blood, or both.

Actually, relatively few snakes are poisonous. About one-fifth of all known species are venomous, and humans are likely to encounter only a score of these. In the United States about one-sixth of the species—20 in 117—are dangerously venomous. About a third of these are quite rare. More important, individuals of these poisonous species are much less abundant than individuals of harmless species—perhaps about one-thirtieth as abundant.

Any snake of this country can be identified as being venomous if (1) it is marked with complete rings of red, yellowish-white and black, the yellow rings bordering

Figure 7. Coralsnake with both red and black rings bordered on each side by yellow. The stippled zone is red, indicated by "R"; the clear zone is yellow, indicated by "Y"; the dark zone is black, indicated by "B."

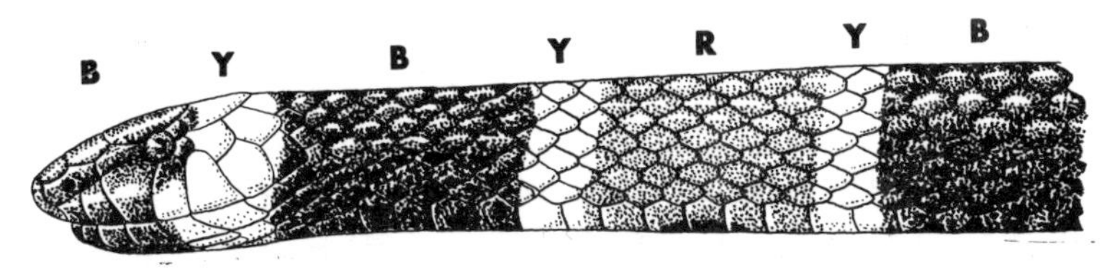

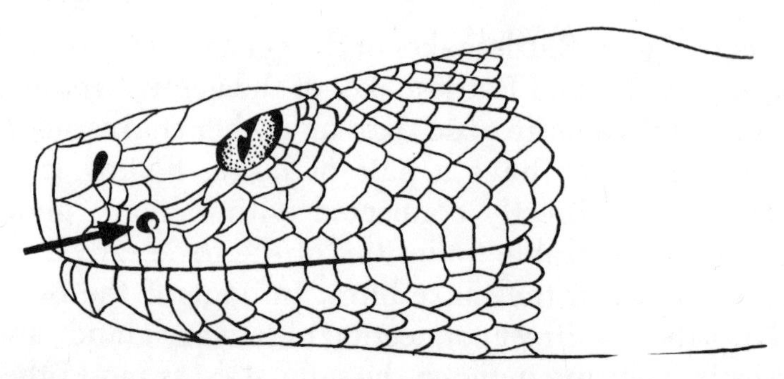

Figure 8. The arrow indicates the pit of a pit viper. The pit is drawn smaller in proportion to associated structures than it actually is. A pit such as this is characteristic of Rattlesnakes, Cottonmouths and Copperheads.

the red on either side ("Red against yellow will kill a fellow; red against black a poison lack"); or (2) it has a rattle at the end of the tail; or (3) it has a deep pit on the side of the head between the nostril and the eye; or (4) it has most or all scales on the under-side of the tail looking just like the broad plates on the belly, not arranged in two rows. Actually, one harmless group of snakes, the Longnose snakes, has a single row of scales under the tail. This species can be recognized as being harmless by the lack of rings as in (1) above and the lack of a rattle or a pit as in (2) and (3) above (see Figs. 7-11).

We have in this country actually only two main groups of venomous snakes: the Coralsnakes, all of which can be recognized by the pattern described above (1), and the pit vipers, which include all of our venomous snakes except the Coralsnakes. This means that Water Moccasins, Copperheads, and Rattlesnakes are all pit vipers. All have the distinctive pit on the side of the head and almost all or all scales under the tail look just like those under the belly—not in two rows as in all non-venomous species, except the Longnose snakes. The vipers have also a large, slender, curved tooth (fang) on each side of the very front of the roof of the mouth. The

Figure 9.
Closeup view of a Rattlesnake's rattle. This photo does not show the "button" at the tip of the rattle, and the knobby section at the end of the rattle is just the part of one segment onto which the following segment was clamped.

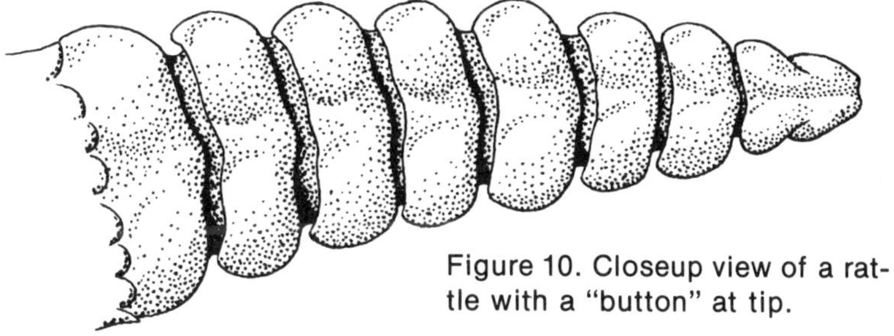

Figure 10. Closeup view of a rattle with a "button" at tip.

Figure 11. Scales under the base of the tail and rear of the belly as arranged in (top) Rattlesnakes and the harmless Longnose snakes; (center) some tropical Coralsnakes; (bottom) many harmless snakes and those Coralsnakes native to the United States. Arrows show the location of the vent. In each case the tail extends to the right.

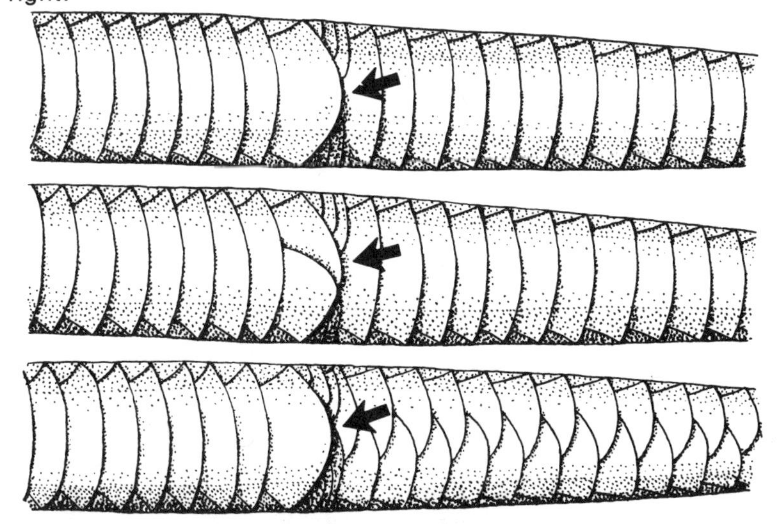

Figures 12 and 13. Two species (*Thamnophis sauritus* above, *Thamnophis radix* below) of the Gartersnake group. Gartersnakes are among the most common—and most commonly captured—of all snake species in the United States.

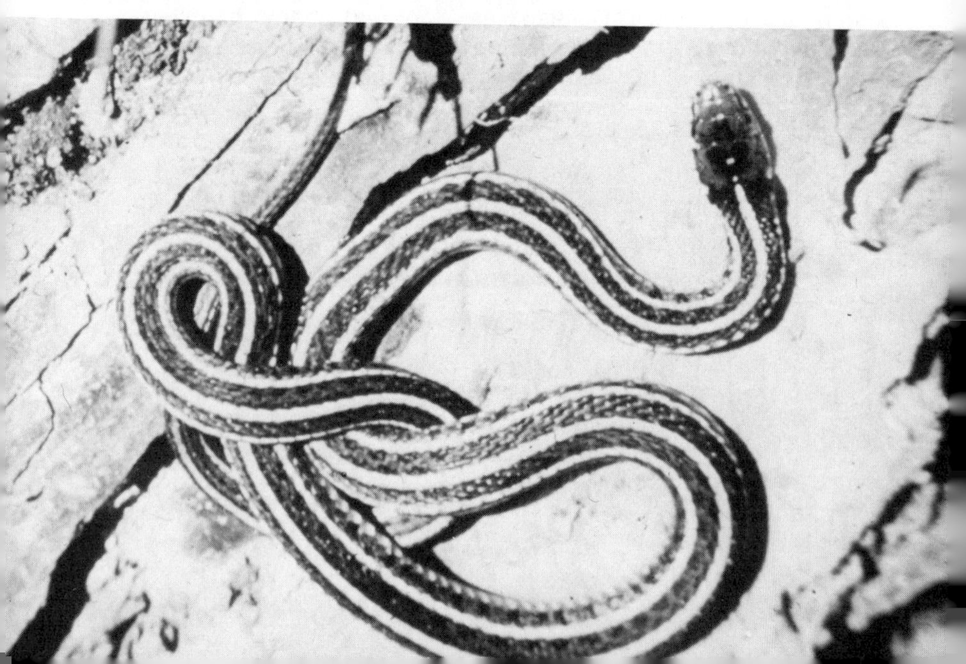

fangs are folded backwards like the blade of a pocket knife when the mouth is closed; they can be swiveled downward into a striking or biting position when the mouth is opened. In the Coralsnakes the fangs are in the same position as in the vipers, but fixed instead of movable, and much shorter—so short as to be easily confused with the ordinary solid teeth which all snakes have.

Groups of Non-Venomous Snakes of the United States

There are 40 native groups of non-venomous snakes in this country, all suitable as pets under certain conditions. Most of them are rather uncommon. Most groups contain several species. The habits are much the same in all species of each group. These different groups will be discussed later. Ordinarily, one would have to obtain snakes of most of these groups either from dealers or by exchange with other snake keepers. A few are so common that they may be found in one's backyard or in small city parks.

The snakes by far the most likely to be collected near human habitations, except in very dry regions, are the Gartersnakes. They are often found in grassy lawns, about fish ponds, in rock gardens and woodlots. They are striped, quick-moving snakes. Fortunately, they can be recognized infallibly by their lined pattern. No poisonous snakes of this country are lined, except as extremely rare variations. Thus, if you repeatedly see plainly lined snakes in damp situations in vacant lots, yards, and about buildings, you may be quite sure they are Gartersnakes or Linesnakes (a close relative) and are safe to handle. When you first catch snakes, it is wise to use gloves. Though small, their teeth are sharp and can scratch or prick rather painfully.

Probably next most abundant in towns are the small Brownsnakes. These are rather nondescript unicolor gray or faintly striped and speckled snakes not more than about 16 inches long. They are active mostly at night; thus in the daytime they would be found chiefly under boards, stones or other flat objects on the ground. They refuse to bite, are totally harmless, and make excellent pets.

Other snakes occasionally found in towns, but more frequently about farm buildings or other places where rats and mice may be plentiful, are the Bullsnakes, Kingsnakes, Ratsnakes, Racers and Whipsnakes. All may serve as pets, but the first two are best. On rare occasions still other kinds may be found in towns. One can never be absolutely certain of identification of snakes found locally, except for the lined Gartersnake and Linesnakes, unless the snakes are checked by an expert or are carefully compared with some manual, such as the field guides by Conant and Stebbins.

The 40 groups of 97 species of non-venomous snakes of this country are listed below, the number of species given in parentheses after each name.

The names following the parenthetic number are the Latin generic names for the group. Each group corresponds exactly with the scope of the one genus cited for it, except for the Blindsnakes, Hooknose snakes, Dwarf Watersnakes, and Boas, which include two genera each. These are real, natural associations, consistent with current taxonomy.

1. BLACK SWAMPSNAKE (1) .... *Seminatrix*
2. BLINDSNAKES (4) ..... *Typhlops, Leptotyphlops*
3. BOAS (2) .... *Lichanura, Charina*
4. BROWNSNAKES (2) .... *Storeria*
5. BULLSNAKE (1) .... *Pituophis*
6. CATEYE SNAKE (1) .... *Leptodeira*
7. COFFEESNAKE (1) .... *Coniophanes*
8. CONENOSE SNAKES (2) .... *Virginia*
9. DWARF WATERSNAKES (4) . . *Regina, Clonophis*

10. FLATHEAD SNAKES (8) . . . . *Tantilla*
11. GARTERSNAKES AND RIBBONSNAKES (13) . . . . *Thamnophis*
12. GLOSSY SNAKE (1) . . . . *Arizona*
13. GREENSNAKES (2) . . . . *Opheodrys*
14. GROUNDSNAKES (2) . . . . *Sonora*
15. HOGNOSE SNAKES (3) . . . . *Heterodon*
16. HOOKNOSE SNAKES (3) . . . . *Gyalopion, Ficimia*
17. INDIGO SNAKE (1) . . . . *Drymarchon*
18. KINGSNAKES (6) . . . . *Lampropeltis*
19. LEAFNOSE SNAKES (2) . . . . *Phyllorhynchus*
20. LINESNAKE (1) . . . . *Tropidoclonion*
21. LONGNOSE SNAKE (1) . . . . *Rhinocheilus*
22. LYRESNAKE (1) . . . . *Trimorphodon*
23. MUDSNAKES (2) . . . . *Farancia*
24. NIGHTSNAKE (1) . . . . *Hypsiglena*
25. PATCHNOSE SNAKES (3) . . . . *Salvadora*
26. RACER (1) . . . . *Coluber*
27. RATSNAKES (5) . . . . *Elaphe*
28. RINGNECK SNAKE (1) . . . . *Diadophis*
29. SANDSNAKE (1) . . . . *Chilomeniscus*
30. SCARLET SNAKE (1) . . . . *Cemophora*
31. SHARPTAIL SNAKE (1) . . . . *Contia*
32. SHORTTAIL SNAKE (1) . . . . *Stilosoma*
33. SHOVELNOSE SNAKES (2) . . . . *Chionactis*
34. SLENDER SNAKE (1) . . . . *Rhadinaea*
35. SPECKLED RACER (1) . . . . *Drymobius*
36. STRIPED SWAMPSNAKE (1) . . . . *Liodytes*
37. VINESNAKE (1) . . . . *Oxybelis*
38. WATERSNAKES (7) . . . . *Natrix*
39. WHIPSNAKES (4) . . . . *Masticophis*
40. WORMSNAKE (1) . . . . *Carphophis*

2. Identification of the Main Groups of Non-Poisonous Snakes of the United States

By means of the following numbered couplets you can find the proper name for any native non-venomous snake you may obtain. To use the key (adapted from Perkins), simply read the statements a and b of couplet 1, decide which fits your snake, and then read off what you find at the right end of the correct half (a or b). Either the name will be given there or the number of the couplet to which you go next in identifying your snake. Continue until you have found a name for your snake.

1—a. Scales on belly same size as scales on back .... **Blindsnake**
b. Scales on belly much wider than scales on back **2**

2—a. One or two pairs of long scales in middle of underside of head **4**
b. No long scales on underside of head **3**

3—a. A plate as large as eye, or larger, in middle on top of head between eyes .... **Rubber Boa**
b. No scales as large as eyes on top of head between eyes .... **Rosy Boa**

4—a. A ridge running down the middle of some or all back scales (look carefully) **5**
b. All scales on back without such ridge **20**

5—a. Scale covering rear intestinal opening (anus)

split obliquely into two scales (look carefully) 6

b. Scale covering anus not divided (see Fig. 11, top and bottom) 16

6—a. Scale at end of snout with a prominent ridge down the middle above . . . . **Hognose Snake**

b. No ridge down middle of scale at end of snout 7

7—a. Only two scales on shortest line between eye and nostril and the rear of these two not conspicuously longer than high . . . . **Brownsnake**

b. Three or more scales between eye and nostril, or if only two the rear one conspicuously longer than high 8

8—a. A scale in middle of head just back of scale at tip of snout 9

b. Two scales just back of snout scale, in contact with each other at about the middle of the head 11

9—a. Five scales bordering upper lip, not counting snout scale . . . . **Conenose Snake**

b. Seven or more scales bordering upper lip, on one side 10

10—a. Two scales along shortest line between eye and nostril; red below, all black above . . . . **Checkered Mudsnake**

b. Three scales between eye and nostril; gray and brown striped above, yellow below . . . . **Striped Swampsnake**

11—a. Two scales along shortest line between eye and nostril 12

b. Three or more scales between eye and nostril 13

12—a. Small, dull-colored, slate, gray or pinkish, with no markings . . . . **Conenose Snake**

b. Larger, brightly striped . . . **Rainbow Mudsnake**

13—a. Not counting the row of large belly scales, 17 rows of scales extending down body at middle of body (half way between head and anus) **14**

b. More than 17 rows of scales at middle of body **15**

14—a. Color above dark, with a light spot on each scale .... **Speckled Racer**

b. Color above greenish .... **Greensnake**

c. Color above black, unspotted .... **Black Swampsnake**

15—a. Ridge down middle of scales on back weakly developed, not easily visible .... **Ratsnake**

b. Ridge down middle of scales on back well developed, easily visible .... **Watersnake**

16—a. Usually four scales in a row across top of head just in front of the three scales between eyes; 27 or more rows of scales at middle of body .... **Bullsnake**

b. Two scales on top of head just in front of three scales between eyes; less than 27 rows of scales at middle of body **17**

17—a. Scale at end of snout very large, looking like a loose patch, with much of edge free .... **Leafnose Snake**

b. Edges of scale at end of snout even with other scales **18**

18—a. Eight or more scales along either lower lip, not counting one at middle on end of chin .... **Gartersnake or Ribbonsnake**

b. Fewer than eight scales along either lower lip, not counting middle chin scale **19**

19—a. Two rows of black spots down belly . . **Linesnake**

b. No spots on belly .... **Conenose Snake**

20—a. Scale covering rear intestinal opening (anus) split obliquely into two scales (look carefully) **28**

b. Scale covering anus not divided **21**

21—a. Broad scales under tail split near middle in two rows **22**

b. Scales under tail like those on belly, not divided . . . . **Longnose Snake**

22—a. Pupil of eye considerably higher than wide, more or less as in a cat **23**

b. Pupil of eye nearly or perfectly round **24**

23—a. Scale at end of snout very large, looking like a loose patch, with much of edge free . . . . **Leafnose Snake**

b. Edges of scale at end of snout even with other scales . . . . **Lyresnake**

24—a. At least one lip scale contacting paired scales on top of snout . . . . **Shorttail Snake**

b. No lip scales contacting scales on top of snout **25**

25—a. Belly and under-side of tail with at least some dark markings **27**

b. Belly or under-side of tail light-colored, without markings **26**

26—a. Back with yellow, black, and red markings . . . . **Scarlet Snake**

b. Back with brownish or grayish blotches . . . . **Glossy Snake**

27—a. Not counting the row of large belly scales, 17 rows of scales running down body, as counted at a point halfway between head and anus . . . . **Indigo Snake**

b. More than 17 rows of scales at middle of body . . . . **Kingsnake**

28—a. Nineteen or more rows of scales at middle of body **29**

b. Less than 19 rows of scales at middle of body **35**

29—a. Two scales along shortest line between eye and

nostril **30**

b. Three or more scales between eye and nostril **31**

30—a. Striped . . . . **Rainbow Mudsnake**

b. Not striped . . . . **Checkered Mudsnake**

31—a. Pupil of eye considerably higher than wide, more or less as in a cat **33**

b. Pupil of eye nearly or perfectly round **32**

32—a. 25 or more rows of scales at middle of body . . . . **Ratsnake**

b. 19 rows of scales at middle of body . . . . **Coffeesnake**

33—a. Three or four scales touching rear edge of eye between scales of lip and big scale above eye . . . . **Lyresnake**

b. Two scales touching rear edge of eye between scales of lip and big scale above eye **34**

34—a. Pattern above of small blotches with one or two series of smaller alternating spots on sides . . . . **Nightsnake**

b. Pattern above of 22 to 26 large blotches, and without alternating spots on sides . . . . **Cateye Snake**

35—a. Two scales along shortest line between eye and nostril, excluding scale of lip and on snout above **36**

b. Three or more scales between eye and nostril, excluding scales of lip and on snout above . . . **41**

36—a. Tail very long (more than half length of body); head long and nose sharp . . . . **Vinesnake**

b. Tail much shorter; head of normal length . . . **37**

37—a. Small scale in front of eye, longer than high . . **40**

b. Small scale in front of eye, not longer than high **38**

38—a. Body without markings back of neck region . . . . **Flathead Snake**

b. Body blotched above **39**

39—a. 13 rows of scales, not counting belly row . . . . **Sandsnake**

b. 15 rows, not counting belly row . . . . **Shovelnose Snake**

c. 17 rows, not counting belly row . . . . **Hooknose Snake**

40—a. Uniform black or brown above, uniform orange below . . . . **Wormsnake**

b. Grayish, often speckled above; cream or white, often speckled, below . . . . **Conenose Snake**

41—a. Scale at end of snout very large, looking like a loose patch, with much of edge free . . . . **Patchnose Snake**

b. Edges of scale at end of snout even with other scales **42**

42—a. Two small scales touching front edge of eye between lip scales and big scale above eye **43**

b. One scale touching front edge of eye between lip scales and big scale above eye **46**

43—a. Lower of two scales in front of eye very small, wedged between eye and lip scale **44**

b. Lower scale not wedged between eye and lip **45**

44—a. Just in front of anus, rows of scales on back and sides number 15 . . . . **Racer**

b. Just in front of anus, rows of scales on back and sides number 11, 12 or 13 . . . . **Whipsnake**

45—a. A light-colored ring around back of neck, or black spots on belly, or both . . . **Ringneck Snake**

b. No ring on neck; no spots on belly . . **Greensnake**

46—a. Green or blue-green in color . . . . **Greensnake**

b. Not green or blue-green **47**

47—a. 17 rows of scales down back and sides, counted at middle of body **48**

b. Fewer than 17 rows at midbody **49**

48—a. Body light brown above; a dark line along sides of head . . . . **Slender Snake**

b. Body black or dark gray above; no dark line on sides of head . . . . **Black Swampsnake**

49—a. Each belly scale with a black edge . . . . **Sharptail Snake**

b. Belly uniformly light in color, or markings, if present, in form of rings encircling body **50**

50—a. Snout normal, rounded . . . . **Groundsnake**

b. Snout flat, shovel-like . . . . **Shovelnose Snake**

The common names given here are not used by all herpetologists. In fact, common names are not as uniformly applied to snakes and other reptiles as to birds and mammals. Some names are widely accepted, others not. A list of common names has been published by the American Society of Ichthyologists and Herpetologists. Most of the names given above agree with that list. Other names are often used in the sale catalogs of animal dealers, particularly since, by most systems of naming, individual species may not bear the name of their group; for example, the Ratsnakes (genus *Elaphe*) include a species often called the Fox Snake (*Elaphe vulpina*, here also called the Womper Ratsnake), and another species often called the Corn Snake. In cases of doubt, the scientific name is the only means of establishing true identity. Note the references on the last pages of this book.

3. The Technique of Handling

We have mentioned the importance of a relaxed, fearless technique in snake-handling. A snake that is to be held comfortably needs support. If it is active at first, let it glide about your arms, hands and body at will. If it glides away from your hands, bring one of them up for support under the forepart of the body, and as the snake moves, keep moving the hands and arms in this fashion. Usually the snake calms down soon and will rest motionless. Repeated handlings will result in a nervous snake's becoming completely docile.

Smaller snakes like to hide, and if allowed to move freely to a comfortable position between the cupped hands, will usually settle down promptly. They can be manipulated later into another position if desired.

All snakes like the warmth of the human body, especially on cool days. They can often be carried for hours inside a shirt.

If a snake is too treacherous to be picked up casually, or if you are suspicious of it, a stick or other object should be used to pin the head gently but firmly to the ground. Then you can reach down with one hand and grasp the snake around the neck and rear of the head. You must be sure to hold the rear of the head, for if the head and any of the neck is left free in front of your hand, the snake can twist its head around enough to bite your finger.

Figure 14. Despite the attractive color pattern of some species, Watersnakes' general irascibility makes them unsuitable in most cases to be kept as pets. Shown is *Natrix fasciata.*

Temperament

Many variations occur in the native nervousness of snakes. Some species are almost invariably quiet, whereas others are almost always nervous. In addition, a remarkable individual variation in temperament does exist; one can never safely predict just how any new individual, whether of a typically tractable or usually nervous species, may act. An occasional specimen of a species normally not offering to bite will remain nervous for weeks after capture, and vice versa. Nevertheless, each group of snakes has a normal or characteristic temperament, despite individual exceptions.

Above:
Figure 15.
Demonstration of the preferred method of picking up a snake by grasping it behind the head to prevent it from biting. The snake is an Eastern Hognose snake, *Heterodon platyrhinos.*

Right:
Figure 16.
Demonstration of approved method of holding a snake (Eastern Hognose snake, *Heterodon platyrhinos*) to prevent it from biting; the herpetologist is Dr. Phillip W. Smith.

Figure 17. Kingsnakes (genus *Lampropeltis*) are generally comparatively large but comparatively even-tempered, making their keeping as pets easier.

The groups of nervous snakes include most venomous species as well as the Watersnakes, Racers, Coachwhips and many others. These hardly make the best pets.

The most tractable large species in this country are, in general, the Kingsnakes, Bullsnakes, Boas, Indigo snakes, Glossy snakes and some species of Ratsnakes. Many smaller species of harmless snakes are docile, but they are more difficult to feed. Many foreign species make interesting pets.

Northern Rosy Boa, *Lichanura trivirgata roseofusca.* Dark stripes are uneven or absent. Rosy Boas are among the most prized snake pets. Occurs in southern California and northern Baja California.

Southern Rosy Boa, *Lichanura trivirgata trivirgata.* Dark even-edged stripes always present. Occurs in southern Baja California.

4. Obtaining the Snake

Snakes suitable as pets can be ordered from various animal dealers in this country. Consult any of the several animal- or zoo-oriented magazines for advertisements of various dealers and their lists of currently available stock, or write them your special wants. Many kinds of snakes can be purchased for less money than a parakeet or a singing canary.

If you possess locally-captured snakes you would like to exchange for others, or if you would like to correspond with other snake hobbyists, you may, provided you are a subscriber, insert suitable brief notices without cost in the news letters of any of the local herpetological societies, of which there are about a hundred around the country. Consult a herpetologist at the university closest to you. All these periodicals carry free notices only for strictly amateur purposes. Business offers of various kinds should be inserted in the regular advertising columns.

A famous connoisseur of snakes observed that in reality most pets, including snakes, are not chosen at all —they simply happen: "Love of animals is so universal that we adopt what circumstances provide and rationalize later." In almost any part of the country one can find harmless snakes that would serve as pets, simply by turning loose trash in vacant lots or about dumps. Logs and stones in or near woodlots and streams will usually yield a snake or two if one persists long enough in searching. In most areas the likelihood of encountering venomous species in the process of searching for pets is very remote. It would be well to consult the nearest authority to learn where to search for snakes without risk of exposure to venomous species.

If you search for your own snakes, take with you a well-sewn cloth bag or two without holes. Sugar sacks are often suitable, but the best are 100-pound cloth feed-bags. Numbers of snakes can be carried safely in such bags, which need only a string tied tightly near the mouth to make them escape-proof. Ordinarily, snake hunters while walking carry these bags tucked under the belt at the sides, and drawn up far enough to keep them from swinging and banging on the legs.

Another useful piece of equipment for the snake hunter is a four-tined or, preferably, a three-tined potato hook. Other garden tools can also be used. Some snake hunters like a single strong hook. Such a hook can be easily made by a blacksmith from an ordinary hoe by cutting the flat parts of the blade away and leaving the central rib continuous with the metal staff attached to the wooden handle. Either the potato hook or the hoe hook will serve for turning stones, logs, brush and trash, and also for holding the snake while it is being picked up.

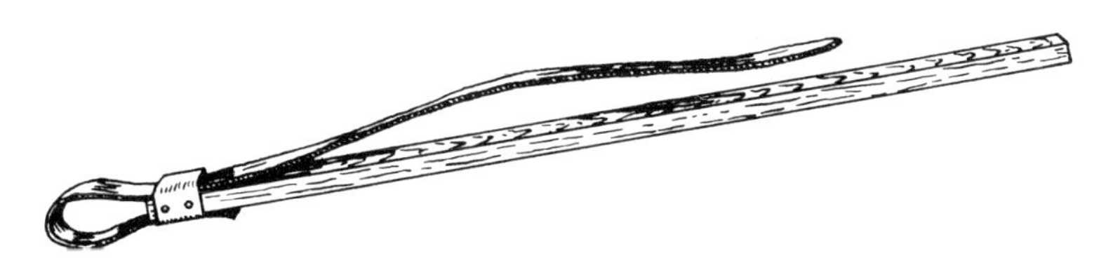

Figure 18. A noose suitable for handling snakes.

Some snake hunters use a noose for capturing snakes. But if made of string or rope the noose may, when tightened, break the neck of the snake as it whips about energetically. A suitable noose should be made of flexible leather strap at least three-quarters of an inch wide (Fig. 18).

Storeria dekayi, a Brownsnake. This small, very gentle snake, widespread in the eastern part of North America, is readily fed on earthworms.

Pituophis melanoleucus affinis, the Southern Divide subspecies of the Bullsnake, native to New Mexico and northern central Mexico.

Pituophis melanoleucus deserticola, the Great Basin subspecies of the Bullsnake. All subspecies of the Bullsnake make excellent pets.

Clonophis (formerly *Natrix*) *kirtlandi*, a Dwarf Watersnake. This docile species readily feeds on earthworms but unfortunately is rare.

Pillstrom Snake Tongs are useful devices for catching and handling snakes; the tongs are available in lengths of 36, 40, 46 and 52 inches.

Anyone hunting snakes where venomous species may be encountered should wear knee boots. These will stop most strikes. Snake-proof boots are sold by many dealers in outdoorsman's supplies. Any knee boots will protect the wearer from most bites.

Anyone striking out on his own to obtain pets or to collect specimens for any reason whatsoever should bear in mind the official exhortations of the American Society of Ichthyologists and Herpetologists as voiced by Dr. Frederick R. Gehlbach, Chairman of the Society's Committee on Amphibian and Reptilian Conservation:

1. That most species of amphibians and reptiles of the United States are suffering rapid decimation of population through both wanton collecting and destruction of habitat;
2. That no one, especially those professing interest in these animals, should be so callous to the urgent need for conservation of all herpetozoa in their natural habitats as to needlessly collect specimens, for whatever reasons, or to damage a habitat by failing to return all overturned cover to its original position;
3. That habitat destruction, mass collecting (especially commercial collecting), and the building of private preserved collections are to be strongly opposed; and
4. That, aside from certain limited observations in captivity, the proper study of herpetozoa is undisturbed in the natural habitat, where most of the scientifically useful information pertaining to behavior, life history, and ecology remains to be obtained.

5. The Care of Snakes

The ABC's of snake care are provision of (1) clean, escape-proof, ventilated quarters, (2) sufficient warmth, (3) an ample supply of clean water, (4) a balanced diet, and (5) prompt treatment of illnesses, deficiencies and infestations.

Housing

Snake cages need not be elaborate. Cigar boxes can be adapted for keeping very small snakes, such as Brownsnakes. A large square hole should be cut in the top and covered with plastic screen. A single strip of adhesive tape will fasten the lid.

Larger snakes (one to two and one-half feet) can be kept in ten-gallon glass aquaria having a wire lid, or in a box. If the depth of a cage (front to rear) is about three-fifths of its width (right to left), the cage will accommodate a snake about twice the width of the cage.

Some dealers supply snake cages, but little labor is required to build suitable cages from material available anywhere. It is easiest to start with a well-constructed wooden box. Especially good are ammunition boxes. With the lid off, a number of holes should be drilled through the sides and the rear walls. The holes should preferably be placed in a row as high above the bottom of the box as possible. If the holes are so large that the snake can crawl through them they should be covered, either on the outside or the inside of the box, with screen. In either case, cover the screen edges with adhesive or other tape. For poisonous snakes, place screen on

Tantilla nigriceps nigriceps, a Flathead snake from southeastern Colorado. A very docile small snake, but difficult to feed. It has tiny fixed rear fangs but is not at all dangerous to man.

Opposite: *Thamnophis elegans elegans,* the mountain subspecies of Western Terrestrial Gartersnake. This is an Oregon specimen. See page 52 for a photo of another subspecies.

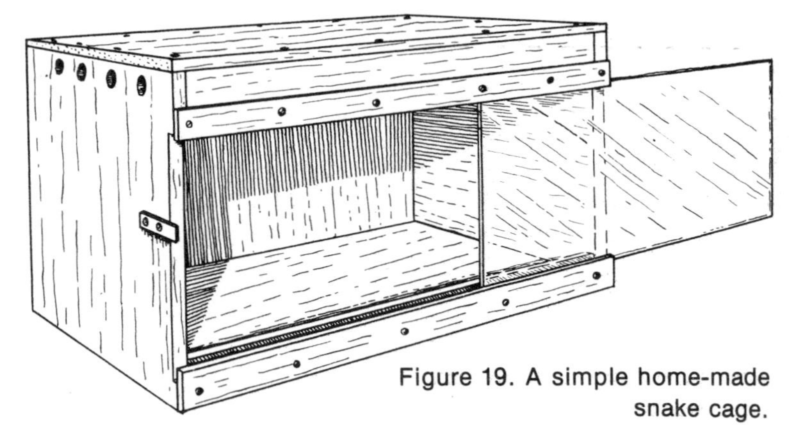

Figure 19. A simple home-made snake cage.

Figure 20. Aquarium tanks are economical, easily available at pet shops and come in a wide range of sizes to suit the size of the snake specimen(s) to be kept. They have the additional advantages of being easy to clean and easy to equip with covers and lighting devices.

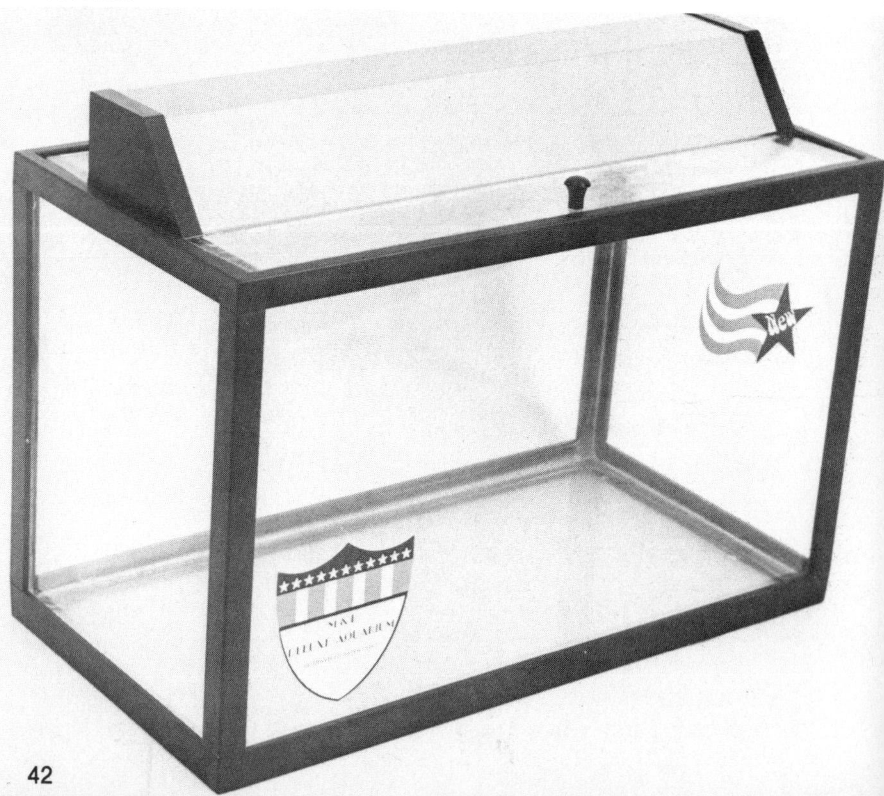

both sides of the holes and use wood at least five-eighths of an inch thick so that the snake's fangs cannot reach through the wire.

Use a glass front. One simple method of installation provides that you saw a narrow edge, only slightly wider than the thickness of the glass pane, off the front of each side piece. The size of the box governs the thickness: double-thickness glass for a large box and ordinary window glass for a small box. Cut the glass to fit freely yet snugly between top and bottom of box, and when in place to reach the outer edge of each side of the box. Now fasten the top on the box. Then get a strip of wood-lath, one-eighth inch to one-fourth inch wider than the boards of the box are thick. Nail or screw a piece of this lath along the entire front edge of the top and the bottom of the box. The glass front will now slide between these laths and the sides. To prevent the glass from swinging inward, tack a guide just inside the glass, either to the top or to the bottom, or both. If the glass is too loose, add strips of adhesive tape to the front of either or both sides.

A suitable snake cage or box should provide: (1) as much circulation of air as possible; (2) visibility; and (3) protection from rough surfaces. Use a minimum of wire-covering, or put it up high where the snakes cannot rub hard against it, since snakes often rub their noses raw on the rough surfaces. This may lead to infection and death, and will at best interfere with feeding. The finer the wire the less the likelihood of injury.

Climbing species may like a few branches braced in the box, but they are not necessary. Wood shavings, sphagnum, Spanish moss, dry leaves, sand, dirt or newspapers are often put in the bottom of the box to facilitate removal of the feces. The feces are semi-liquid when deposited, but in a few hours in a dry cage become a nearly odorless mixture of a few dry, undigested

Thamnophis sirtalis fitchi, the Valley subspecies of the Common Gartersnake, from Oregon. The several western subspecies of *Thamnophis sirtalis* characteristically have bright red areas between the black spots on the sides. See pages 45 and 52 for photos of other western subspecies.

Opposite:
Thamnophis sirtalis concinnus, another western subspecies of the Common Gartersnake.

parts and a powdery white substance, uric acid (comparable to the urine of mammals). When dry the excrement can easily be removed by scraping. In the absence of a liquid urine and in the lack of odor of the feces, snakes resemble birds, to which they are somewhat related.

Care should be taken to prevent ingestion of rough, indigestible objects along with food: wood shavings, for example, can kill the snake by splintering and working through the wall of the stomach or intestine. If rough materials are used as a floor covering the snake should be fed in another, bare-floored cage.

A receptacle into which the snake may retire out of sight is welcome for virtually all species, although it is not necessary. A small box open at one end will do, if the cage is large enough to hold one that is in turn large enough to hold the coiled snake. For small specimens a piece of bark, cardboard, or light plywood under which they may crawl is adequate.

A rough stone too heavy for the snake readily to move is a very desirable item in the cage. It serves chiefly as an aid to loosening the skin when it is ready to shed.

Temperature

Sunshine is not essential for the welfare of snakes, provided theirs is a well-balanced diet. In fact, snakes are easily killed by overexposure to the sun. The chief value of sunlight lies in the warmth it affords to snakes when they are cool. However, you can provide warmth more safely by artificial light, which you can easily install in or near the cage, and fit with an electric bulb (which you may safely leave bare) of a wattage which through experimentation you have found will keep the cage between 75 and 85 degrees F. To keep the cage temperature more or less uniform, you can attach a

Figure 21. Lighting units for aquarium and terrarium tanks sold in pet shops are available in a number of different styles. Some cover the entire top of the tank, and some (called "strip reflectors") cover only a portion of the top.

thermostatic control. However, this is not essential provided you keep a thermometer in the cage and check occasionally to make sure the temperature is neither too high nor too low. In warm weather you may have to leave the bulb off permanently.

During winter the snakes in most parts of this country hibernate in the ground. In captivity, even when inside temperatures are comfortable for ourselves, snakes usually go into a hibernating routine, becoming inactive and refusing food. Snakes in good condition can go without food for weeks or months without harm. If kept cool during the winter, as in a basement at temperatures of between 40 and 55 degrees F., they can be covered and should not be fed. They must not be allowed to dry out. With approaching spring the snakes can be returned to their preferred activity temperatures of from 75 to 85 degrees F., and should accept food as usual.

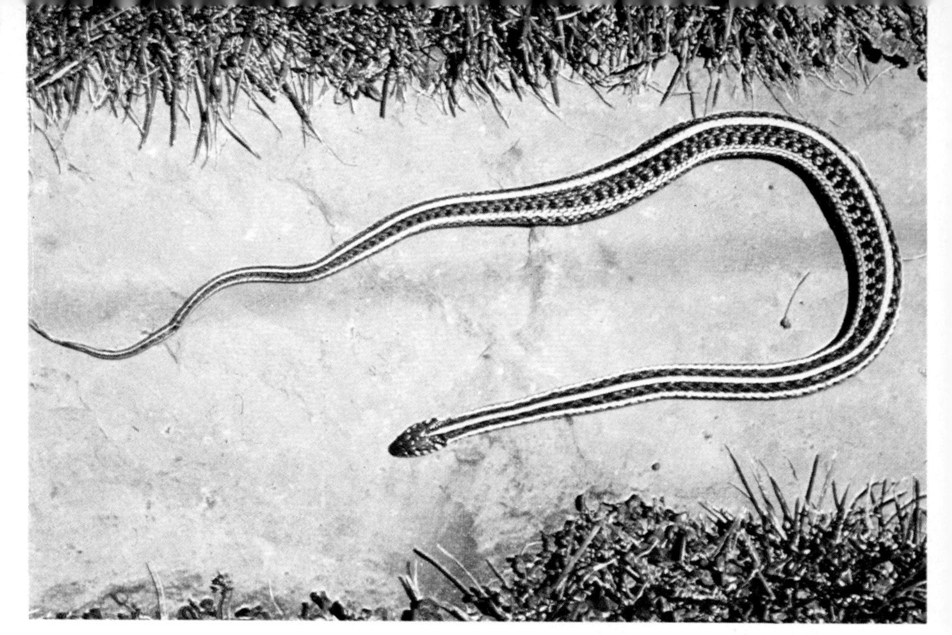

Thamnophis radix haydeni, the western subspecies of the Plains Gartersnake, widely distributed and often common in the prairies of central North America. This specimen is a pregnant female taken in Colorado.

Thamnophis sirtalis sirtalis, the eastern subspecies of the Common Gartersnake. Unlike the western subspecies (see pages 44 and 45 for photos of western subspecies), the eastern subspecies has no red in the pattern.

Thamnophis proximus, the Western Ribbonsnake, one of the snakes in the Gartersnake group. Its close relative the Eastern Ribbonsnake (see Figure 12) has a dark line along the edge of the ventrals.

Thamnophis cyrtopsis cyrtopsis, the Black-necked Gartersnake, from an Arizona specimen.

If you must keep your snakes at normal room temperatures during the winter, they will very likely be too cold to eat readily, and yet be too warm for their stored fat to keep them until the return of warm weather. Should your snake refuse to eat and become thin, you may have to force feed it a few times, even though the low temperature will not provide ideal conditions for digestion and assimilation. Preferably keep your snake either at the proper activity temperature of from 75 to 85 degrees F., and feed it regularly, or at the hibernating temperature, and do not feed it at all.

Water

Water must be provided at all times, as it is needed not only for the snakes to drink but also for bathing. Most snakes need to soak their bodies in water occasionally, especially before shedding. The bath before shedding is especially important under conditions of captivity, since the diet may be deficient in certain components otherwise necessary. On the other hand, excessive humidity is undesirable for most species. Plenty of room should be allowed for the snake to crawl into a dry place. For very small snakes the water container should be very shallow, else they will not find the water. Snakes drink like horses, by sucking water between the lips, held below the water.

Feeding

Although slighted by nature in many ways, having no limbs, no outer ears, no eyelids and no vocal cords, snakes have one unusual gift: an enormous mouth. The snake's jaws, joined loosely by movable bones and muscles, can stretch wide to engulf food several times the size of its head. But the snake has no teeth designed for chewing. It must swallow everything whole. Anacondas and Giant Pythons, which on rare occasions may reach a length of 35 feet, may as an extreme fast as long as four years. Large snakes of most species reaching a length of six feet or more have been kept as long as a year without food.

Food constitutes the most important obstacle to keeping snakes. Most species require live food. Training them to take more easily obtained food is usually a tedious chore. Snakes can be force-fed, but not successfully on a long-term basis. Individuals frequently have very fixed food preferences and are difficult to break of them. A good example is a 14-foot King Cobra that was once received at the Brookfield Zoo in Chicago. This species normally eats other snakes, but this specimen repeatedly refused live and freshly killed offerings, and had grown thin in starvation. Eventually it was discovered that frozen snakes warmed-over were taken readily. After that, no difficulty was encountered in feeding the Cobra, which soon was in excellent condition.

Sometimes snakes with strong preferences can be hoodwinked into accepting other food by disguising it as the preferred food. Watersnakes and some Gartersnakes, which eat only fish, will sometimes take dead mice or strips of meat if they are first rubbed with fresh fish. As these snakes are guided chiefly by odor, they will accept these substitutes on the basis of odor and despite differences in texture.

Non-venomous snakes used as pets fall into two categories according to their manner of subduing prey: constrictors and non-constrictors. There is a very sharp line of distinction between the two groups. The constrictors live chiefly, but not exclusively in all cases, on warm-blooded animals (birds and mammals), which they kill not by crushing the prey to a pulp, but simply by retarding the rhythmic (or, near death, the spasmodic) movements indicative of life—breathing and

Thamnophis sirtalis pickeringi, the Puget Sound subspecies of the Common Gartersnake. The narrow dorsal stripe and dark sides are characteristic. See pages 44, 45 and 48 for other subspecies.

Thamnophis elegans vagrans, the Wandering subspecies of the Western Terrestrial Gartersnake; pictured is a Colorado specimen. See page 41 for another subspecies.

Arizona elegans, the Glossy snake, a species of constrictor related to the Bullsnake. Nocturnal; fares well in captivity.

Opheodrys aestivus, the Rough Greensnake. This diurnal insect-eating species is difficult to keep in captivity. Try feeding it daddy longlegs, which captive individuals of the Smooth Greensnake readily accept.

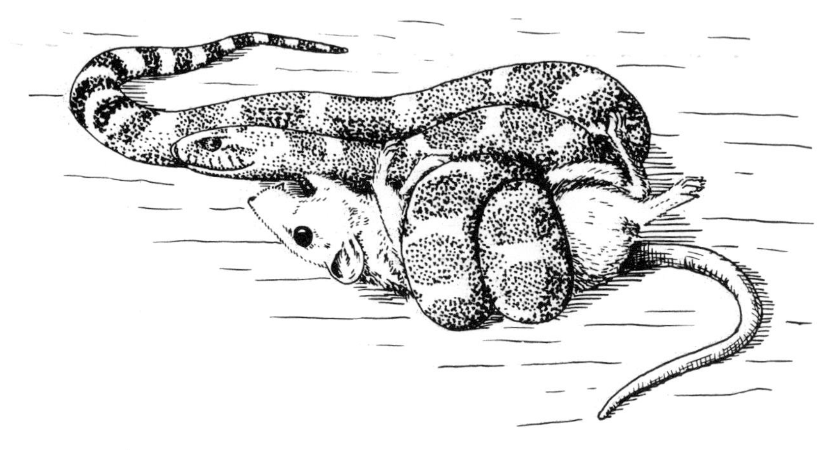

Figure 22. A Bullsnake killing a rat.

heart-beat (Fig. 22). Shortly after movements cease, the snake uncoils, carefully checks its prey to be sure it is dead, then proceeds to swallow it. Constriction follows naturally with the stimulus of pulsating movements, as can be proved by rhythmically flexing the muscles of the arm as a pet snake, such as a Kingsnake or Bullsnake, is entwined about it. Despite the large size (eight feet or so) which these snakes may reach, they are not dangerous as constrictors even to a child: an eight-year-old can remove one from any part of the body with ease. The power they can generate is negligible to man, efficient though it is in killing rats, mice, gophers and the like. Only the giant constrictors, such as Boas and Pythons, may be considered at all dangerous, but only at lengths of nine or more feet.

The non-constrictors simply catch and swallow their prey, in some cases using the body to hold it down. For the most part, they live on cold-blooded animals—frogs, fish, lizards, and snakes.

Both constrictors and non-constrictors include so-called "cannibalistic" species, which eat other snakes of the same or different species. Such snakes are better termed "ophiophagous," since cannibalism by literal definition involves eating members of the same species. The predator may devour a snake as large as, or even larger than, itself. One should not cage cannibalistic snakes with other snakes, unless for feeding purposes, or unless the cannibal is much the smaller.

As a rule, snakes should have food once every week, although small individuals may require it as frequently as every other day. They should not be stuffed, even if they take the food voluntarily. If they skip one feeding, or even several, ordinarily no harm results, provided the snakes are in good condition to begin with.

If a snake refuses its usual food of live birds or mice, they may be placed in a small box in the cage. The box should have a small opening through which the snake can crawl. In this way a temperamental snake

Figure 23. A constrictor species (shown is a Speckled Kingsnake, *Lampropeltis getulus getulus*) grasping its prey, another snake; even constrictor species do not attempt to constrict comparatively very small prey.

Heterodon platyrhinos, the Eastern Hognose snake, shown with only the head and neck spread; the forepart of the trunk also can be spread. Despite the fierce bluff, this is a docile snake—but not easy to keep in captivity. It needs frequent feedings and prefers toads. See also Figures 5, 15 and 16.

Opposite:
Sonora episcopa episcopa, the Great Plains Groundsnake; shown is a Colorado specimen. This attractive, completely docile snake is rather difficult to feed; in nature it eats insects, spiders, centipedes, millipedes and scorpions.

can often be induced to feed. Care should be taken to make sure that the mice or rats do not turn the tables and attack the snakes. Sometimes snakes which refuse to feed refuse also to defend themselves. Then mice or rats can seriously injure or even kill them. It is advisable to train snakes to eat freshly-killed animals.

Unless they are very tame, snakes like privacy while eating. Having introduced the food, one should go away far enough so that one's movements will not disturb the snake.

Diet

It is not sufficient that a snake merely receive a given volume of food over a given period of time. That food must supply all its dietary needs for good health and long life. The most common dietary deficiencies are the same as for man: vitamins and minerals. A young snake in particular needs extra large quantities of calcium and phosphorus for bone-building. Since many snake infections center in the skin, it is essential to keep the skin vitamin (C) up to par. Snakes that eat other vertebrates, for example birds, mice, other snakes, lizards or whole fish, get a diet balanced in all respects with these foods. Earthworms also seemingly provide a balanced diet.

Some kinds of insects, however, are clearly inadequate by themselves to provide a balanced diet; lizards fed steadily on any one type of insect, such as mealworms or flies, often develop serious dietary deficiencies. Provision of supplementary foods in such cases is essential for maximum success with captive animals.

When vitamin and mineral intake cannot be kept high enough in foods taken by the snake, they should be provided in synthetic or prepared form, mixed with the food as a powder or liquid. Cod liver oil is an excellent supplement but may not provide all needed components of the diet. Capsule vitamin-mineral supplements are excellent for medium-sized and larger snakes, since the capsules may be opened and the contents sprinkled on or wrapped within the food.

If foods are readily available only seasonally, or if it is desirable to obtain large quantities of food that cannot be kept alive until eaten, the modern kitchen is supplied with a device made-to-order for the problem—the deep freezer. Most snakes can be trained to take dead food as well as live food, and in general this is a safer procedure since risk of injury is eliminated. However, the food should not be spoiled. If it is frozen at once after killing, it can be kept fresh in any quantity. Mice, toads, frogs, snakes, lizards and chicks can be kept and a few thawed just before feeding. If the food is moist, wrap it in separate packets of wax paper or else it will be difficult to remove portions at feeding time.

Freezing is very useful also for prepared foods such as strips of meat, cutting the strips in advance and wrapping them separately for use. One expert in snake-keeping first cuts thin slices of meat of the proper size, then adds a sprinkling of vitamins and fine bone meal (available from most pet shops), rolling up the slice with the food supplements inside. He makes up a large quantity of these food "pills" at one time, stores them in his freezer, and each weeks thaws the desired number for his snakes.

Obtaining the Food Supply

The most critical hurdle in keeping any snake as a pet is supplying proper food. For insect-eaters, it is possible to collect large quantities of insects when they are abundant in warm parts of the year, freezing them for storage. Grasshoppers and crickets can often be collected by hand. Insects of all sorts can be gathered in large quantities by "sweeping" with an insect net. Many

Heterodon nasicus nasicus, a Western Hognosed snake; shown is a specimen from Colorado. This snake is a docile toad-eater, but it needs frequent feeding. See Figures 5, 15 and 16 and the color photo on page 57 for illustrations of the eastern species.

Heterodon nasicus nasicus playing possum; note the gaping mouth and dangling tongue. Once it is inert after briefly writhing as though in the throes of death, the snake can be lifted and will remain as limp as a piece of rope. If tossed onto its belly, however, it will quickly turn itself belly up.

Lampropeltis getulus floridana; this Kingsnake is a mouse-eater and is one of the most prized of all pet snakes.

Lampropeltis getulus californiae. This subspecies, like all other Kingsnakes, makes an excellent pet. Some individuals are longitudinally striped rather than ringed.

kinds can be attracted to light at night; if a funnel leading into a jar is suspended below the light a pure culture of insects can be obtained. Do not offer pillbugs, true bugs (the insect orders or suborders Hemiptera and Homoptera) or lacewings as food, because they are very distasteful and may discourage the snake from trying to eat at all.

Earthworms may be picked up in large quantities on rainy or wet warm nights. They may be kept alive for a time in a container of loose earth mixed with dead vegetation, but to store them over winter, it would be well to freeze them, wrapping them separately, otherwise they will stick together. I am not certain that thawed earthworms would retain their consistency well enough to be acceptable, but it would be worth trying. Great care should be used not to feed snakes the small red manure earthworm, which is poisonous enough to kill many small species. In this age of extensive use of insect and weed poisons even the common earthworm (*Lumbricus terrestris*) is dangerous to use as snake food, because the worms, which are not very sensitive to these poisons, may carry in their bodies concentrations sufficiently strong to kill snakes, which are sensitive.

Some types of insect food are available commercially. Mealworms and crickets can be purchased from dealers. An article by H.S. Swingle, listed in the References, gives full directions for raising crickets yourself. Cockroaches and mealworms also may readily be raised by the pet owner. Directions for raising cockroaches can be found in the article by Tarshis (1961). Mealworm culture is briefly described in a leaflet distributed free by the Bureau of Sport Fisheries and Wildlife (see References under that name, 1962b); this leaflet also describes the essentials of collecting and care for numerous other snake foods, as for example catalpa worms, frogs, salamanders, minnows, mice, earthworms, crickets and cockroaches. Two books available at pet shops, book stores and libraries are *Live Foods for the Aquarium and Terrarium* and *Encyclopedia of Live Foods.*

The Tarshis cockroach-rearing technique works well in rearing crickets, although Norma Rothman (see References, 1962) reports "good luck at the Institute for Cancer Research keeping the commercially available cricket *Acheta domestica* in aquaria covered with cheesecloth (wire screening could be used, or perforated aluminum). The straw in which the crickets are packed is left in the aquarium for the crickets to climb on. Bread crumbs are sprinkled liberally on the floor of the aquarium together with rolled oats. Pieces of bread, apple or potato may also be given. Water is supplied with daily fresh lettuce, and shallow large petri dishes (or saucers) containing absorbent cotton soaked with water are placed at each end. Crickets desiccate easily, but seem to have difficulty finding a dish of wet cotton if there is only one in a large aquarium, hence moisture-containing foods or dishes must be very readily available. They also drown easily, so there must be no standing water." Cockroaches, crickets and mealworms alike may develop an infestation of insect mites. These mites can be controlled by introducing into the quarters several small blotters impregnated with a 0.5 per cent solution of a poison called *Tedion.*

Fish are readily procured from dealers either live or frozen. Since fish-eating snakes are guided largely by odor and not by shape or movement, strips of fish are just as acceptable as whole live ones. The simplest procedure is to procure frozen fish and to cut strips from it. It is also simple to seine minnows and freeze them (wrapped separately to prevent adherence together) for a reserve supply. Undoubtedly small whole fish are preferable to strips of large fish in supplying a complete diet.

Lampropeltis triangulum, the Eastern Red Kingsnake, one of the most beautiful of American snakes. It feeds on snakes, lizards and small mice, but only at long intervals. Although the pattern of this snake much resembles that of the venomous Coralsnakes, note that the red rings are bordered in black; in Coralsnakes the red rings are bordered by yellow.

Phyllorhynchus browni browni, the Saddled Leafnose snake, from Arizona. Note the weird patchlike snout and the very large blotches. This lizard-eating species is strictly nocturnal.

Toads and frogs can be purchased alive in spring from dealers and frozen to provide a year-round supply. In spring they can often be secured locally at night by hunting with a flashlight at breeding assemblies.

Baby chicks can be obtained from hatcheries in spring; culls are especially cheap and just as acceptable as prime stock. Sparrows may be caught by hand around buildings on a dark night, using a flashlight. They can also be trapped, or caught in a "mist net" hung where they commonly fly. The latter technique is especially convenient and productive.

Before attempting to catch any wild animal, examine the conservation laws governing the area in which you live.

Mice and rats may be trapped for food and supplied either dead or alive. White mice, rats or hamsters can be purchased from dealers either to be fed directly or used in maintenance of a breeding stock. A free U.S. Department of Agriculture Leaflet, 253 (see References), gives directions for maintenance of colonies of these animals. Sometimes it is possible to obtain feeding or breeding stock from local colleges, schools, or hospitals where excess experimental animals are often available.

Whatever the natural diet, any snake will digest raw meat, and if properly fortified this suffices as the sole food. The only difficulty is persuading the snake to accept it. Some snakes do not question the naturalness of the offering but accept it at once. Others can be trained to accept it either by withholding other food or by disguising the substitute as the real thing: earthworm, frog, fish or mouse odor can be imparted to the meat by rubbing these animals on the meat or wrapping them together for a period of time. Many snakes are so completely dependent upon odor that a fish-eater, for example, will quite happily accept a piece of meat that smells like fish. It is even possible to disguise mice as fish, although not all snakes can digest mice as well as their natural food.

Assist-Feeding

Snakes that are too weak or too stubborn or too spoiled to feed by themselves can be "assist-fed" by any one of several means. "Assist-feeding" includes any sort of aid by the owner in the feeding process other than actually putting the food, whether specially prepared or not, into the snake's quarters. It is convenient to recognize three types of "assist-feeding": at one extreme is *force-feeding*, at the other *active hand-feeding*, and in between *passive hand-feeding*. The terms "active" and "passive" refer to the degree of participation by the snake in the feeding process. There is no sharp distinction between these three sorts of assist-feeding, but most procedures fall readily into one category or the other.

1. Force-feeding is the insertion of food into the stomach against the recipient's will, commonly by use of dull forceps, a pencil or some other object to push food into the esophagus, then gently massaging the food with the hands into the stomach, located about one-third the distance from the head to the base of the tail. Normal or nearly normal foods may be used, as for example dead mice, rats, fishes or birds, or parts thereof. Strips of fish or other meat may be substituted. At best this is a very tricky procedure; great care must be exercised to avoid rupturing the delicate walls of the esophagus. Only in exceptional cases, when all other devices have failed, should force-feeding be adopted.

2. Passive hand-feeding involves use of a feeding-gun of some sort. This may be simply a glass tube and a cone rolled from strong paper, plastic or cloth. More complex devices (see Fig. 26) are an all-plastic caulking gun, or a specially designed dual plunger apparatus. In

Figure 24. A colony of cockroaches. When feeding insects, especially insects that are usually regarded as household pests, to pet snakes, be certain that the insects have not been exposed to poisons used as pesticides. To be completely safe, the snake keeper must maintain his own colonies of food insects.

Figure 25. Closeup of a cricket, one of the common insects often used as food for insectivorous snake species.

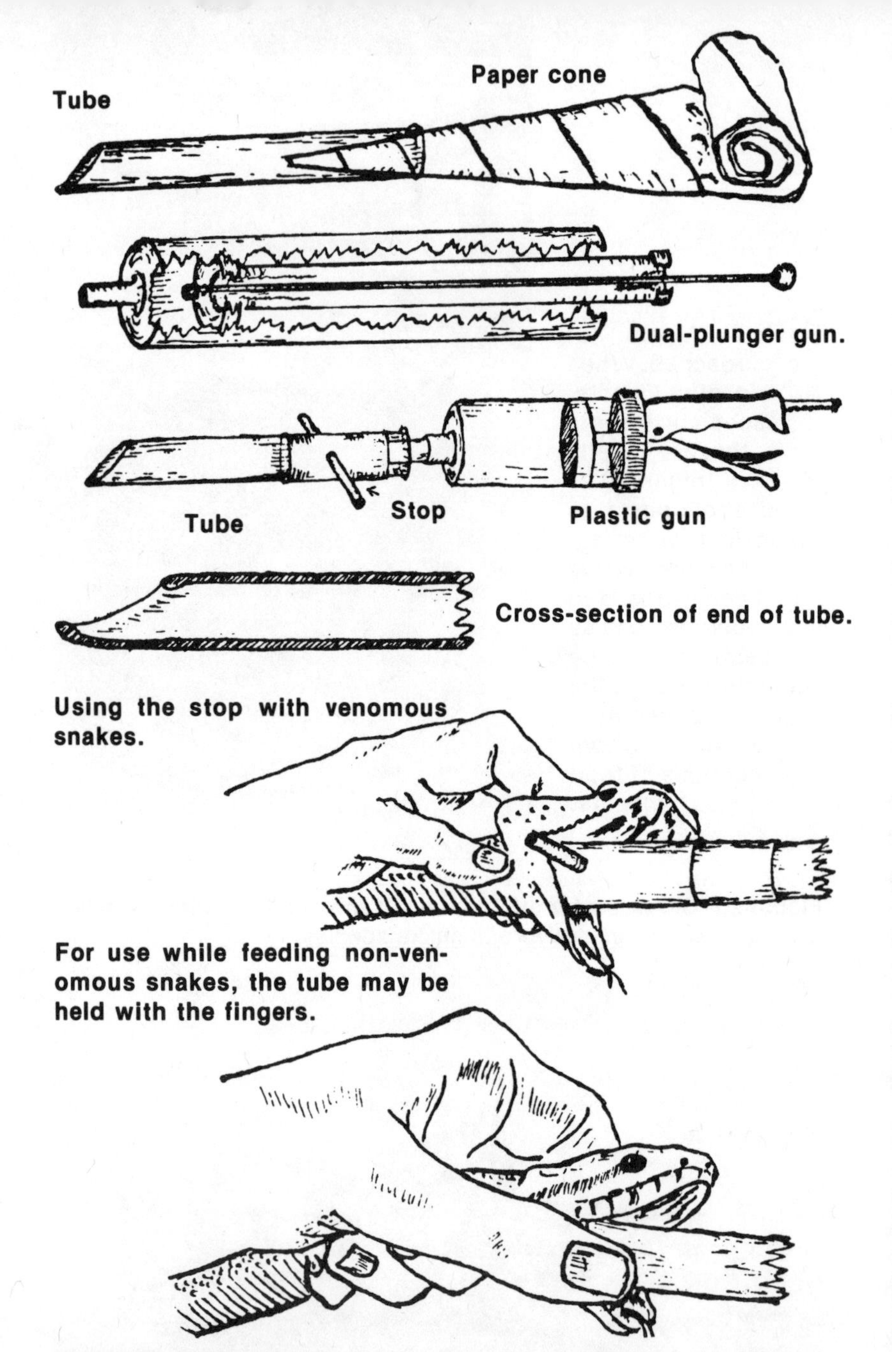

Figure 26. Food-injection devices and their application. From top to bottom: a simple tube and cone, a dual-plunger injection apparatus, and an all-plastic caulking gun.

this system, the tube is the most important component. Pyrex glass is often preferred, its end shaped as shown, to plastic because its smooth hard surface prevents possible damage to delicate teeth or throat membranes. Its diameter should be the same or slightly larger than the neck of the specimen, with limits of approximately 3/8-inch to 3/4-inch when using a meat mixture. A smaller tube may be used when feeding a liquid meal. Length should be no more than 10 inches for the largest specimen. The adjustable stop is most convenient for feeding venomous reptiles without accidentally snagging a fang.

Mix the ingredients and load them into the barrel of the gun. Attach the tube, coat it generously with cod liver oil or Vaseline, and insert it slowly into the snake's mouth and throat. Squeeze the gun slowly until the desired amount is injected, then remove it. Leave the tube inserted if you want to swab the mouth or check for evidence of disease. The tube is then withdrawn slowly as the fingers close the throat behind it. The food may be eased farther toward the stomach by gently stroking the snake's belly. Wash and sterilize equipment before reuse.

Although care in loading the gun will keep trapped air in the mixture to a minimum, there is bound to be some, and "burping" may result. It is no cause for alarm.

Rompell reports food mixtures have been used with equal success: "As a basic formula, to one pound of finely ground lean beef or horsemeat add one egg, one teaspoon cod liver oil, one teaspoon calcium, eight drops multi-vitamin mixture, and whatever medication may be indicated. In lieu of the calcium and cod liver oil, two tablespoons of a powdered food supplement, which contains all the essential minerals, vitamins and brewer's yeast, may be more convenient.

"Highly recommended is the use of any natural

foods, such as fish, rodents, chicks or insects, put whole through a meat grinder or blender and used as above."

Rompell's methods have been successful on everything from an eight-inch *Diadophis* (Ringneck) to a 15-foot Python, as well as on crocodilians, lizards and amphibians. "A word of caution; there is a disadvantage in continued use of hand feeding. An eight-foot Central American Boa (*Constrictor constrictor imperator*), in excellent condition, has been with us for years. She will endure an occasional two-month fast, but being spoiled and lazy, she steadfastly refuses every inducement to eat until she gets her dinner in a tube. If you do not want to be a sausage-stuffer, be sparing in the use of hand feeding."

3. Active hand-feeding involves exertion by the snake in swallowing. The owner's participation is confined to placing the food in the mouth or holding it where the snake can engulf it. The following experiences of Barbara Froom in caring for a Smooth Greensnake are especially illuminating (see References).

"Beautiful and gentle though it is, the Smooth Green Snake is best not kept in captivity. Although some authorities say it makes a good pet for children, others stress that it refuses food and languishes. This is usually the case. In nature its chief foods are spiders, crickets, grasshoppers and smooth caterpillars and grubs. Children are indeed well able and eager to search for such food for their pet during the summer, but what happens in the winter? In most cases this type of food is not obtainable and if the snake is considered a pet one does not want to put it into hibernation.

"My chance for experience in caring for this species occurred more than two years ago (September, 1960). The snake, a 16-inch female approximately two years old, was found in Ontario's Algonquin Park. It is rare in that district. The snake had been displayed by the

Department of Lands and Forests along with other Ontario snakes at the Canadian National Exhibition. Since I work for the Department I became 'nursemaid' for the little Green Snake at the end of the Exhibition.

"I housed her in a terrarium with sand, rocks, driftwood, water dish and a flower planter at one end. The plants could be watered without the rest of the snake's home becoming damp. She shared the terrarium with two small Ribbonsnakes born at the C.N.E. Although she did not appear to be in bad condition, and had recently shed, she was quite thin. The ability of snakes to fast is overemphasized—small snakes in particular must be fed regularly and often. She needed nourishment immediately, so I filled a medicine dropper full of blood from a roast of beef, tilted back her head and pressed the dropper to the opening between the lips. I released drop after drop and she drew in the blood without opening her mouth. This method had worked the previous year when I had to give a laxative to a garter snake.

"I offered her all the natural food I could find, but she ignored everything, even spiders and smooth green caterpillars. I also tried mealworms. I continued to blood feed her daily. Had it been my own snake I would have released it, but such was not the case, so I was able to put into practice a theory I have long believed to be true.

"I force fed the snake food completely foreign to its natural diet: small minnows, strips of raw beef, fish, earthworms and even bits of raw chicken heart. It would be more accurate to call this unconventional manner of feeding assist feeding. I simply opened her mouth with my thumb nail and inserted the food well back of the glottis, an operation that took some practice before I could manage without help. The snake would then swallow the food normally, 'walking' over it with her jaws. It appears that the automatic swallowing reflex was triggered, hence no forcing of the food down the esophagus was necessary.

"In order to get sufficient food into the snake at one feeding, I quickly added another small minnow, piece of meat, etc., before the tail of the first minnow disappeared and so on until she had three or four 'helpings.' My reptiles (five snakes, two Japanese turtles) are treated as pets, not specimens. I am not a collector, but am very interested in the psychological aspects of these creatures. They seem to have more intelligence than they are credited with, and this is displayed frequently under good care. In the case of my 'greeno' I don't think I can call her swallowing an automatic reflex. More and more she demonstrates an ability to refuse what she does not like, which, fortunately, is very little. She is now taking good-sized minnows, and raw beef is eagerly consumed, but she is repelled by earthworms and it is even difficult to open her mouth when a worm is offered.

"The results of this method have been gratifying. The snake grew rapidly and her color became a rich emerald green. At first she was completely unresponsive, unlike my alert Garter and Ribbonsnakes. She soon began to take an interest in exploring the terrarium, sunning herself, and rushing from her hiding place when I fed the Ribbonsnakes. She would sniff at their fish and come to my hands for food, but would not voluntarily open her mouth to take it. Her mouth is in excellent condition.

"Recently she has taken a few green caterpillars, small spiders and a large cricket on her own for the first time. However, she soon ignores this natural food and I have to resume the assist feeding. She will sleep soundly for two or three days after a meal, then appear to be searching for more. Generally, I feed her every second day or whenever she comes to my hand appearing hungry. Except prior to skin shedding I do not let her go for more than a week at the most without food.

"It is my opinion that any snake, no matter what its natural diet, can be fed in this manner, the swallowing reflex being brought into action without the food being forced down the gullet. . . However, if the snake will cooperate and take the food once the mouth is opened, minnows or larger fish (in the case of bigger snakes) may be easily passed down the gullet with little effort compared with trying to force down a whole mouse or rat. If an insect eater such as mine can digest fish, there seems to be no reason why a rodent eater cannot assimilate them. Of course only liquid should be given after a prolonged fast, or if the snake is ailing, until it is sufficiently restored to digest solids.

"Unless it is necessary to keep a snake for a specific purpose, no method of unnatural feeding should be resorted to. The snake should be released in its own habitat and within its natural range, if it will not feed voluntarily."

6. Habits of Snakes

Time of Activity

Some snakes are active only during the day and sleep at night. The Racers, Indigo snakes and Greensnakes are good examples of this type. Most other species are active chiefly at night, or in the late afternoon. Watersnakes, Gartersnakes, Linesnakes, Brownsnakes and all poisonous snakes belong to this group. During the day, nightsnakes ordinarily hide in some burrow or crevice, or under some object. In cool weather, however, even they are likely to be found abroad during the day, if the sun's rays are strong enough to warm them a little.

Whether nocturnal or diurnal, all snakes sleep several hours during every 24-hour period. They sleep with their eyes open, for they have no movable eyelids. And because they cannot close their eyes, they are easily disturbed. For this reason every cage should have a suitable retreat where the snake can sleep in peace.

Molting

Snakes molt the thin outer skin layer at various intervals. While some species molt only once a year, most others molt three or four times a year. If a snake is healthy and can soak its entire body in water to soften the shed layer, the molt (often called a "skin," but actually only a part of the skin) is shed in one piece. Injured snakes tend to molt more frequently. The molt is started backwards around the snout, and by rubbing against various objects it is pulled backwards, wrong side out,

Figure 27. A snake molting. The enclosure used to hold a pet snake should be provided with an object having projections on which the snake can snag the layer of skin to be shed, thus making the shedding operation easier.

over the entire length of the body. The snake actually crawls out of the shed layer.

Failure to shed usually leads to skin infections and a general debilitation. Snakes which do not shed properly by themselves should be helped by hand. It is important that all parts, especially the eye covering, come off. When the latter fails to shed, it often becomes opaque, and unless a subsequent molt removes the abnormal tissue, permanent blindness results.

Approximately a week before molting, the eyes become clouded, remaining so for four or five days. Since the snake can see only dimly during this time, it usually is inactive and irritable. Then the eyes clear, and in two or three days the outer skin-layer loosens and should be shed. Now is the time to make sure that the molt has been effected properly.

It is often assumed that molting is a function of growth, much as in insects. This is not the case. Mature, slow-growing snakes molt at the same rate as young ones. The molt serves to replace worn skin, which in nature is subject to unceasing abrasion as the snake moves about.

Fighting

Snakes, as a rule, are not strongly combative. A few species are ophiophagous, eating their own and other species. Racers, Whipsnakes, Indigo snakes and Kingsnakes are pronounced snake-eaters. They subdue their prey either by constricting it or by holding it with their bodies while swallowing it.

Non-ophiophagous snakes molest one another but little. Conflicts, if such they may be called, consist of a peculiar dance-like ritual of intertwining bodies that would scarcely seem effective as a means of combat. The snakes literally seem to wear each other out, but curiously enough do not bite each other during the conflict.

Senses

The tongue of a snake is a soft, pliable organ with a forked tip. Its chief function is to serve as an accessory smelling organ. It picks up airborne particles and carries them into the mouth, where they are received by Jacobson's organ—the actual sense organ which detects the odors.

The tongue is used differently under varying circumstances, suggesting other functions not now known. In feeling about a possible food object, the tongue is protruded only a very short distance. In locating a probable source of food in the near vicinity, the tongue is rapidly flicked in and out of the mouth. Then when the snake is on the defensive and highly keyed to respond to every indication of danger, its tongue protrudes and is held almost still, moving up, then down, its tips sometimes dilating and then drawing together. Just what purpose is served by the latter action is not known. Odor detection is the objective in the first two situations, but in the third something else seems to be involved.

The eyes are keenly attuned to movements which are quickly detected even though they may be slight. Still objects, however, are not readily recognized.

Day-prowling species tend to have particularly acute eyesight, and find their food chiefly by this means. Nocturnal species tend to rely very little upon eyesight to find food, but are guided, often to ludicrous extremes, by odor alone. A Watersnake will try to swallow its own tail when that organ has been rubbed with fish, which it very much likes.

Figure 28.
A snake (Brownsnake, *Storeria dekayi*) with tongue extended.

Snakes do not respond to airborne sound waves. They have no outer ear, and the middle ear is degenerate. The inner ear, which detects the actual sound, is capable of registering sound waves, and has recently been proved to do so, equalling the sensitivity of a cat within the range of 100-500 cycles per second. Nevertheless only sound waves received by the body through the ground produce a visible response. That means snakes can respond only to low tones carried by the ground. This limitation does not prevent them from detecting the approach of a person, even when they cannot see him.

7. Reproduction and Breeding

Snakes ordinarily mate in the spring. The males court the females by gently rubbing their bodies, especially the chin, against the females. Usually the mating process lasts several hours, with little or no movement by either animal. Snakes (and lizards) are different from all other vertebrates in having two copulatory organs (hemipenes), either one but not both of which may be used in a single mating (therefore more appropriately termed paripenes). Snakes are faithful to neither their mates nor their young. Males frequently breed with different partners during one mating season.

In areas where snakes of any given species are rare, encounters between potential mates may not occur every year. Thus a mechanism has evolved whereby females can retain the sperm from one mating alive in minute pouches inside their bodies for up to at least seven years. Most reptiles share this capacity for one mating to suffice for fertilization over several seasons—a vital adaptation for species whose individuals may be widely scattered and have limited means for finding each other. Annual mating is advantageous even in these animals, however, for the viability of the sperm diminishes steadily although slowly, so that only a small percentage of the eggs are fertile after a mating that occurred five or more years earlier.

How Snakes Reproduce

Most snakes lay elongate eggs, depositing them in moist burrows, in logs, in the ground, or in piles of debris (see Fig. 29). Others—Watersnakes, Gartersnakes, Brownsnakes, Linesnakes, Swampsnakes, Boas, Conenose snakes and the pit vipers—give birth to their young. In either case, the young are hatched, or born, in late summer or early autumn. Except in rare instances, the mothers show no interest in either eggs or young after these have left their bodies.

Ordinarily, snakes reproduce every year, but not always. Some few species reproduce regularly every other year, at least in certain (northern) parts of their ranges.

Breeding in Captivity

Since snakes become quiescent and lazy in captivity, they are difficult to breed. Zoos sometimes succeed by providing ample space, an ideal temperature and the right sort of food. Individual fanciers should keep their snakes in the best possible condition. Males and females

Figure 29. A clutch of snake eggs.

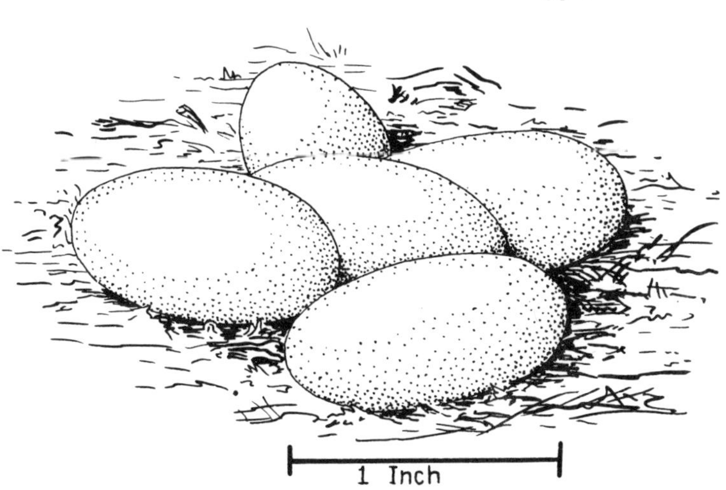

can be kept together throughout the year. They should be of approximately the same size. Males may be distinguished from females by their proportionately longer and more gradually tapering tail, which is thicker toward the base than in females. In case of doubt, snakes 18 inches long or longer can be sexed by probing with a slender, blunt, slippery object just inside the rear edge of the anus. In males, the probe will readily slip into a pocket on each side, passing a short distance into the hollow copulatory organ. In females there are no such structures.

In the case of live-bearing snakes, no special preparation for the birth of the young need be made. In the case of egg-laying species, a box of damp straw may be provided. Careful watch should be kept on the female and the eggs removed soon after they are laid, for they should be inspected daily for molding.

Hatching Eggs

If your pet snake should lay eggs in captivity, or if you should get them elsewhere, they can be hatched

Figure 30. The "combat dance" of Copperheads, a behavior presented by males of many snake species when competing for territory or mates. The snakes do not bite each other, but they intertwine their bodies while rising steadily higher in a sort of Indian wrestling with their bodies.

with the proper care. They should be placed in a small open dish with damp paper-toweling under and over them. This dish should be placed in a larger covered dish containing water. The idea is to keep the eggs moist, yet to allow free movement of air about them. Eggs placed in damp soil or sand, although seemingly in a natural setting, usually mold and spoil. Two months or more may be necessary for the eggs to hatch although for snakes in general the range of variation is from four days to about four months. Other techniques are described in the article by Zweifel, listed in the References.

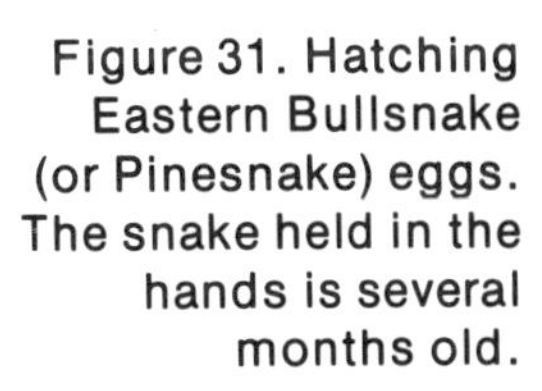

Figure 31. Hatching Eastern Bullsnake (or Pinesnake) eggs. The snake held in the hands is several months old.

Just before hatching, a snakelet cuts a slit in the thin, leathery shell of its egg by means of a tiny "egg tooth" on the tip of the snout. The egg tooth is shed shortly after the snake hatches and is never replaced. The snakelet cautiously pushes its head through the slit, patiently inspecting the surroundings and withdrawing the head if movements disturb it. After a few hours the hatchling usually crawls out of the shell, but if disturbed it may remain within its embryonic home for days.

How Fast Snakes Grow

Snakes grow astonishingly rapidly during the first

Figure 32. Young Racer, *Coluber constrictor,* probably of the subspecies *Coluber constrictor flaviventris,* the Blue Racer. All Racer subspecies are spotted in the young but become unicolor above in the adults. The eastern subspecies (see Figure 34) becomes black in adults, whereas others become bluish, blue-green, speckled white, etc.

Figure 33. Young Yellow Ratsnake, *Elaphe obsoleta quadrivittata.* The young of all Ratsnakes (*Elaphe*) are blotched; in some kinds the blotched pattern is retained throughout life, whereas in others the pattern becomes striped or unicolor above, either dark or light.

Figure 34. Adult Black Racer, *Coluber constrictor constrictor.*

Figure 35. Adult Yellow Ratsnake, *Elaphe obsoleta quadrivittata.*

few years. Small species reach maturity during their second year, and nearly their maximum length in two or three years. They may grow afterwards, but only very slowly. Larger species may require three or four years to reach maturity and continue to grow fairly rapidly for another similar period. Even the giant constrictors, such as Pythons and Boas, reach maturity in only four or five years, attain a near maximum size in eight or 10 years, and afterwards grow very slowly.

How Long Snakes Live

Small species of snakes, one to two feet long, are thought to live a maximum of approximately eight years. Larger species, such as Bullsnakes and Kingsnakes, are known to have reached an age of 15 years, and may live 20 years, or a little longer. Even the giant constrictors are not known to live longer than approximately 30 or, at most, 35 years. In any species which ranges widely in temperate regions, northern specimens tend to live longer under natural conditions than southern specimens.

Changes in Pattern

The color markings (pattern) of many species of snakes are different in the young and in the adults. Young Racers and some Whipsnakes are blotched, whereas adults are more or less striped or unicolor. The Painted Watersnake and Cottonmouth also are blotched in the young, but dull-colored in the adults. Even in species showing no marked pattern changes with growth, a difference in brightness of the pattern and in the general tone may be expected.

Young vipers have a very light-colored tail-tip, which seems to be a decoy for possible prey, such as mice. As the snakes grow larger, this tip assumes the dull coloring of the rest of the tail.

8. Diseases and Parasites

Snakes are commonly distressed by mites and mouth infection. Specimens just purchased should be carefully examined for tiny mites under the scales or about the eyeballs. These pests are no larger than the point of a fine pencil lead. If not brought under control, mites will multiply rapidly and kill the snake. Furthermore, an infested cage or container will harbor mites for months, even though no snakes may have occupied it. A snake placed into formerly infested unsterilized quarters is likely to develop a mite infestation.

Fortunately, mites may be killed in any of several ways. One is by use of Dri-die, a completely non-toxic fine powder which dehydrates mites and their eggs (see the article by Tarshis, 1960, in References). A snake placed in a box or bag with this powder will be rid of its mites within a half hour. The powder can be sprinkled in the corners of the cage to kill mites that might be hiding there. If the pests reappear, repeat the treatment. Dri-die is available not only in pure form but also in a flea powder; the mixture is toxic to snakes and should not be used. Another useful mite control is "Vapona No-Pest Strips," a flypaper impregnated with volatile toxic compounds to which external parasites are susceptible, snakes and other reptiles less so. A square inch suspended for 24-48 hours in the cage suffices to kill the pests.

The common mouth infection ("mouth-rot") produces a light-colored substance which prevents complete closure of the mouth and renders breathing difficult. The teeth become loose, the gums apparently tender, and the snake refuses to eat. If not treated, the infection will kill a snake within one to three months. Fortunately, it can be completely controlled with one to three applications of a two and a half per cent aqueous solution of sulfamethiazine (sold under the tradename of Sul-Met). The solution is applied with a medicine dropper to all surfaces of the open mouth.

Snakes occasionally suffer from respiratory diseases. These and most other bacterial or viral infections, local or general, can be treated successfully, and with-

Figure 36. Many ticks have parasitized this captive snake; the ticks attach themselves to their victim by burrowing under the scales and sinking their hold-fast organs into the flesh, leaving their posterior portions exposed.

out harmful side-effects, with antibiotics developed for human medication. Terramycin, streptomycin, and penicillin are suitable for use on snakes.

Intestinal upsets, similar to serious constipation, will sometimes kill snakes. The abdomen becomes swollen and taut, and as the snakes move they tend to roll on their sides or back. They seem reluctant to bend the body. Except for manual elimination of the intestinal plug, no treatment is known. Responsible for the difficulty is usually an excessively large deposit of uric acid in the rectum, which can be forced out by gentle massage.

Now and then soft blisters appear on the skin of snakes—an often fatal condition, for which no reliable control is known. Bathing in Sul-Met may be beneficial, at least if the blisters are opened. Likewise, baths with ethyl alcohol at strengths of between 40 and 55 per cent may prove helpful. A common recommendation is that the blisters be opened and the interior sterilized with a good antiseptic. Excessive dampness, which seems to be associated with some blister diseases, should be eliminated.

In the mouth of some snakes worms may occasionally be seen, but since apparently they cause no serious damage they may be disregarded. No snake parasites or infections, contrary to certain afflictions of pet mammals and birds, can be transferred to man—another good reason for preferring snakes as pets.

Several excellent pamphlets, books and articles about the ills of captive reptiles have appeared in recent years. They are summarized with full references in Murphy's indispensable booklet (see References).

9. Taming and Training

Perhaps the most accomplished tamer of snakes of all time—certainly in this country—was Grace Olive Wiley, a very gentle little lady who died some years ago (1948) in California from the bite of one of her pets which had not yet been fully tamed. In order to raise money to feed her animals, this nearly penniless animal-lover was attempting to pose a newly acquired Cobra for a magazine writer, when the snake turned and struck her.

Miss Wiley tamed Rattlesnakes, Coralsnakes, Sea-snakes and many other kinds. Her special interest was in venomous species. Her specimens became totally at ease, some breeding and bearing their young for the first time in captivity. The magnitude of her achievement is measured as much by the notorious nervousness of most venomous snakes as by the poisonous properties themselves. Cobras and Mambas are recognized as the worst of the lot, but even these she mastered. Patient, lengthy observation and careful adjustment to the snakes' reactions were the simple basis of her almost uncanny ability to handle snakes. There was no magic involved.

Certainly the average person does not care to devote the time and care to making pets of snakes that Grace Wiley did, but from her and many others we can learn that even a little attention will yield results. The quieter species require much less attention than most other kinds of pets. And any snake, approached properly, can be tamed.

Some well-known groups of people give the generally false impression of taming venomous snakes. The Oriental snake fakirs "charm" Cobras, which appear to be trained and to sway to and fro in their erect stance with spread hood, facing their piping owners. Some of these fakirs sew their snakes' mouth shut with fine thread invisible from the ordinary observer's distance. Others do nothing to their snakes, but simply become delicately attuned to the snakes' reactions. Mistakes are usually fatal. The paces through which some "charmers" put their snakes are amazing, and certainly not understood by the average man.

The Hopi Indians of our own Southwest perform an annual snake dance during which "priests" handle venomous Rattlesnakes with abandon. These snakes have recently been shown to have their fangs carefully removed. They are reluctant to bite without them. If a bite were to occur, the danger from it would be considerably lessened.

In our eastern mountains of Kentucky and Tennessee, a fanatic snake-cult uses venomous snakes in religious ceremonies. Treatment of bites is prohibited, and from time to time members die from the effects. Apparently no attempt is made to subdue the snakes or to prevent them from biting. That they do not bite more frequently may be attributed to the relaxation and lack of fear their handlers exercise.

Finally, there is a remarkable snake cult in Africa that has acquired a reputation for having reached maximum knowledge of snake psychology and control. Its priests can successfully treat bites of highly venomous Cobras, and confer immunity to snake bite by a secret process whose hocus pocus conceals a technique closely approximated by the processes used in the preparation of antivenin. This cult contributes one of the most intriguing chapters to the history of the relation of man and snakes (see the book by Carnochan and Adamson in the References).

Hedged with superstition and fear about snakes, the unsuspecting person falls an easy prey to erroneous statements about them. Unfortunately, 90 per cent of the sideshow and roadside zoo pitches are fictitious. Most so-called snake-tamers do no more than any average person could do if he would forget his unjustified fears. On the other hand, factually sound, informative and fascinating lectures are given by snake keepers in such reputable exhibits as the Black Hills Reptile Gardens in Rapid City, South Dakota, and Ross Allen's Reptile Institute in Silver Springs, Florida.

Training of Snakes

Although the casual observer may think snakes are unresponsive, unaware of the hands that provide for them and incapable of showing intelligence, he would be surprised at the similarities of their responses to those of more conventional pets such as mammals. It is commonly said that Cobras are the most intelligent of snakes. Certainly the hatchlings are as quick and alert as a mouse, and zoo men are certain that the adults learn to distinguish keepers and respond to handling much as mammals do.

That snakes are susceptible to training of some sort is evident by their quickly learning not to bite. They also exhibit surprisingly delicate sensitivities if they are observed carefully. Barbara Froom of Toronto, Canada, suggests some of these evidences of responsiveness:

"More than six years ago, I got my first gartersnake, Bijou, when he was about 10 inches long (he is now 32 inches). This snake has been the tamest, friendliest creature one could imagine. He always comes out of his hut when I enter the room, will drink from a cup, and will take a good variety of food items from my hand while I hold him on my lap. He loves to have the back of his neck scratched and often objects when I place him back in his terrarium. As we lack a spare room, my snakes are in my own room. They are completely used to me and are frequently handled. This would be impossible with a venomous snake, for taming requires complete lack of fear by the handler. Those who scoff at the pet value of gartersnakes are missing a great deal as far as serpentine psychology is concerned. Freedom from fear, and simplicity of feeding and housing, are facts often overlooked by over-eager young herpetologists, who are all too anxious to have either exotic or venomous snakes.

"In two years, Bijou was joined by Bettina, another gartersnake, about 12 inches in length. Bettina, of course, is also tame, but does not enjoy as much handling as Bijou. This snake is a somewhat fussy feeder, not taking readily to such things as chicken hearts, raw beef, etc., unless they are first scented with fish. . . Bettina is very gentle and I can place food right into the mouth without my finger being so much as scratched. I had to teach Bijou when he was young not to strike at his food. He would lunge out violently at a piece of fish or beef, whereupon I would withhold the food, give him a gentle slap, then hold the food right up to his mouth. He finally caught on and the only thing he will strike out at now is live minnows.

"Perhaps the strangest experience I had with Bijou was his unusual reaction to my two little Japanese pond turtles when I first bought them. He was in such a state of panic, apparently from the scent of the tiny turtles, that he started to emit strange whimpering sounds upon exhaling his breath, he quivered violently when near the turtles and in a few days went into some kind of a convulsion, twirling about on his back with his head bent backwards. This actual twirling, according to a veterinarian who examined him at the time, could have been the result of having eaten too many minnows, which might have produced a toxic effect. I was able to save him by keeping him in a cool place (where the contortions seemed less violent) and giving him milk of magnesia to get rid of any possible toxicity. Bettina acted agitated in the presence of the turtles but displayed no such reaction as Bijou. When the snakes were taken to the cottage the following summer, I noticed Bijou's nervousness at the apparent scent of a native turtle that I had temporarily at the far distant end of the veranda. Although he did not twirl about, he commenced lurching about in the portable screen cage and breathing heavily. I noticed that Bijou was so content in captivity that anything of his natural environment seemed to frighten him. I posed him on a setting of rocks and driftwood for photos and he went rigid—seemed scared and breathed hard. Neither he nor Bettina showed any desire to want to escape from their cage. . .

"I have raised two ribbon snakes from birth and for two little creatures born at the same time of the same mother, one can hardly believe there could be such a difference in personality. Bows eats just about anything and everything (as far as snake food goes) including earthworms, is so fat he looks like a little viper and is bold and doesn't object to handling. Buttons is shy, continually hiding behind the planter, is skinny as the result of being a very fussy eater and hates to be handled in any way. They are now more than two years old, about 27 inches in length and get along well with the gartersnakes."

Snakes are capable of learning, and therefore can be trained. But their responses to stimuli are limited and unpredictable, and their motivation for self-gratification is slight. Snakes quickly learn that certain types of prey can be dangerous. In Chicago's Brookfield Zoo a 14-foot King Cobra that was in no mood to eat once was chewed in shipment by a smaller but fierce Indian Rat snake. The Cobra thenceforth shied away from all live snakes, regardless of size or species, despite the fact that snakes are its only food. It would have starved had it not been discovered that it would accept snakes that had been frozen, then thawed. It would not accept even freshly killed snakes!

Likewise a normal mouse- and rat-eating viper may be so frightened by the bite of a hungry rodent that it will never molest a live mouse or rat and must be fed dead ones. Once such a fixation occurs, it is virtually impossible to change—not even by the threat of death. A snake which has learned to fear mice will not even defend itself from one, though it could readily kill it if it wished. Thus in captivity a single hungry or thirsty mouse occasionally kills even a large snake.

Similarly, a snake with adequate food and water will become accustomed to a mouse caged with it and will not eat it even though it readily accepts newly-introduced mice. But if the mouse is removed and later re-introduced, the snake cannot recognize it and will accept it readily as food.

Grace Olive Wiley was justifiably proud of the way she had trained her snakes to accept her without fear, even snakes of the most deadly and nervous species. They would act naturally in her presence, breeding and producing young. In addition to accepting their keeper, snakes have learned to anticipate food when feeding is regular and to use one area or the water dish for defecation.

Linda Bowman of Rochester, N.Y. reports (by letter) that all of her Watersnakes and Gartersnakes are "house broken" to the extent that they always defecate in the dishes of warm (65° F.) water provided about eight hours after eating. They do not then return to the dish until it is cleaned out. Some are trained to eat dry dog food, and almost all—even Greensnakes, Ringneck snakes, Cornsnakes, and Gartersnakes—have learned to accept strips of lamb and stew meat.

So unresponsive are snakes to experimental designs applicable to birds or mammals that evidence on their ability to discriminate color is conflicting. Some experiments suggest that they discriminate fairly well, whereas others indicate very poor color recognition.

The Price of Being a Snake Fancier

Snakes are generally regarded as peculiar animals. They are! People who keep them are thus likely to be looked upon as being peculiar or mere sensation-seekers. Neither reputation is enviable. Unfortunately, both viewpoints are sometimes true. Yet even the harshest critic is curious about the unknown and strange. Curiosity is universal, and there is nothing unnatural about satisfying a practical curiosity. One can satisfy that curiosity about snakes much more easily than many persons think. There is no need to conceal your efforts, but any showing-off will only backfire.

In keeping snakes, as in handling them, one must act naturally and relaxed. There is satisfaction enough in simply learning what snakes are really like and how they live, without making a conspicuous show of one's hobby. Furthermore, our willingness to learn something concerning snakes is one more step forward in developing a tolerant, balanced perspective—always a mark of growth and of maturity.

The Basis of Fear of Snakes

The pronounced, even irrational and fanatic, fear many people have of snakes is so impressive as to suggest an instinctive source for this reaction. Yet there is absolutely no real basis for such a belief. The fear reaction is learned from others. Children and adults who have not been taught to fear snakes will maintain nothing but a warm, lively interest in these fascinating creatures.

The snake is often taken as a symbol of sly wickedness—as perpetuated by the Biblical story of the Garden of Eden. But in that story the snake is used solely as a symbol—a symbol based on familiar human experience. That experience shows not that snakes are wicked, but that they are essentially noiseless in movement, surprise easily, are often quick to strike, and can be deadly. These features by themselves are not unique to snakes, and cannot account for the special fear reserved for them. Tigers, leopards and other predators are equally stealthy and deadly, but they are respected as well as feared. Snakes are not generally respected; man seldom sees anything at all admirable in them. Many theories have been advanced in an attempt to account for man's fear of snakes. The most plausible theory is the combination in them of "lowliness," stealth and potential deadliness. I agree with Kauffeld and Conant that sex plays no role in the fascination snakes hold, and that the fear of them is learned in early youth from elders who fear snakes. The ignorance which for centuries fostered this fear made quite natural the selection of a snake as the symbol for lowly stealth in the story of Adam and Eve.

Modern enlightened education is, however, gradually producing some effect in dissipation of ancient fears. TV programs, biology classes and nature centers are all trying to educate youngsters to understand and appreciate all wildlife, including reptiles. They try to teach children which snakes are poisonous and which are not, counteracting parents who, in trying to protect their children, condemn all snakes.

Fears of snakes take many forms. In the thousands of years they have been associated with man, snakes have been credited with bizarre powers: the ability to heal, to bewitch, to suck milk from cows, to flail enemies with the tail, to roll into a hoop and pursue prey at

Figure 37. Youngsters can handle snakes even as large as these seven-foot Boas (*Boa constrictor*) after the snakes have been given frequent handling during a few weeks in captivity.

Tropidoclonion lineatum, the Linesnake, small, drab, docile species easily fed with earthworms. The underside of this snake is brightly marked with two rows of large black dots. The specimen shown is from Colorado.

the speed of a cheetah, to swallow their young and disgorge them when danger has passed.

Snakes can do none of these things. Many other strange and false superstitions have arisen about snakes. In reality, most characteristics from which arise man's distrust of snakes are really the result of snakes' adaptation to their environment. They are inconspicuous, in part for the sake of camouflage that is essential because of their relatively slow rate of travel (maximum seven miles per hour for even the fastest snakes). The rearing, spreading, hissing and even much of the striking are merely desperate defensive devices for making the snakes appear dangerous. Bluff is used to the maximum degree. With rare exceptions, snakes strike only when startled, cornered or seeking food.

10. Selecting Your Pet Snake

What makes the most desirable snake pet? The answer depends on what facilities are readily available. Ideally, the best pet is the one that most quickly learns not to bite under any circumstances. In actual practice, however, the best snake pet is the one that combines gentleness of behavior with ease of feeding. Many otherwise ideal pets are unsuitable for the average person simply because of their difficult food requirements. Food is the first essential to consider in keeping snakes. One should select a pet snake which is at least fairly easy to feed, for troublesome feeding soon sours one on his hobby.

Owing to the importance of food availability in the choice of a snake pet, the common pet species are grouped below according to food preferences. Furthermore, these groups, including their respective species, are arranged in order of pet value, the most desirable listed first. The grouping is limited to domestic species and includes all non-venomous kinds.

The Worm Eaters

Among the most satisfactory pet snakes are the worm eaters. These snakes rarely or never bite human beings, and so they make safe and trustworthy pets for children. While bites from non-poisonous snakes are sel-

Rhinocheilus lecontei lecontei, the western subspecies of the Longnose snake. This snake is a lizard- and mouse-eater and is not easily kept in captivity.

Opposite, above:
Hypsiglena torquata ochrorhyncha, an Arizona specimen of one of the six Nightsnake subspecies in the United States. This snake is a mildly poisonous but docile lizard-eater.

Opposite, below:
Hypsiglena torquata, the Nightsnake, shown in the process of laying an egg. Note the slitlike vertical pupil, the mark of a species whose retina is adapted for night vision, even though the snake often emerges during the late afternoon daylight. The narrow pupil protects the retina in bright light; in darkness, the pupil is wide open (round).

Figure 38. Earthworms of different sizes and species; earthworms are excellent food for worm-eating snake species and may be cultivated with comparative ease to assure a steady supply—but care must be exercised to make sure that red manure worms do not become mixed in with the culture of non-toxic earthworms.

Figure 39. Mealworms, larvae of the beetle *Tenebrio*, are shown here with two adult beetles and two pupae.

dom serious, they often induce worry over possible infection as well as surprise and pain. With most worm-eating snakes such concerns are unnecessary.

Earthworms, which are the principal food of these snakes, are usually easy to get throughout the year, except in winter. If well fed up to this time, the snakes should be able to go without food, especially if they are kept covered with moist earth and kept cool. But if the snakes overwinter in a warm house, their metabolic rates are so high that reserves will not last through the long cold season.

If worms cannot be obtained, assist feeding may become necessary. Small strips of meat may suffice, or an occasional mealworm. As a matter of fact, these snakes might possibly be induced to eat mealworms, as well as earthworms, by simply covering the former with earthworm slime. Since they select their food chiefly by odor, they probably will eat mealworms so treated. By gradually reducing the amount of slime, the snakes might take the mealworms without any earthworm flavoring.

Only the common species of nightcrawlers should be used. The red manure earthworm, as well as some other species, are not acceptable and may be even poisonous to the snakes. They should not be mixed with the common nightcrawlers. I have had snakes die shortly after eating mixed worms. When not mixed, the undesirable worms are flatly rejected by the snakes. The common nightcrawler is easily recognized by its large size, its occurrence in gardens, lawns and fields, and its color. The undesirable species are smaller, more wiry, often differently colored, and seldom found in lawns or gardens, except in compost heaps. Nightcrawlers may be made available even during droughts by regular and thorough sprinkling of a small plot of soil after dark.

The most dependable among the worm eaters are

Salvadora hexalepis hexalepis, the Western Patchnose snake. Note the large triangular scale on the tip of the snout; the scale is similar to but smaller than the scale on the snout of the Leafnose snake (see page 64). The specimen shown here is somewhat emaciated. This racer-type species is rather omnivorously carnivorous.

Adult (above) and young *Coluber constrictor.* The adult represents the Blue (midwestern) subspecies; the young Racer below probably is of the Black (eastern) subspecies. Compare with Figure 32.

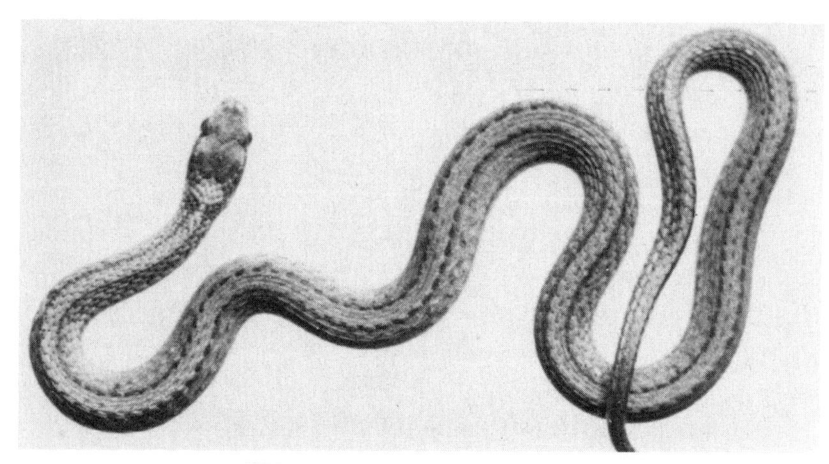

Figure 40. Red-bellied Brownsnake, *Storeria occipitomaculata*, a colorful but small docile species easily raised on earthworms.

the BROWNSNAKES (*Storeria*) of two species: the Redbellied Brownsnake and the Dekay Brownsnake. I have never known either to bite. Neither exceeds 16 inches in total length, and the average is about 10 inches. The Redbellied is the prettier, having usually a salmon-pink venter, but all look much alike above, with their rather dull, gray-brown color. The back may have faint light stripes or scattered dark flecks.

The lack of beauty is compensated for by complete docility; these are quiet, gentle snakes which do not nervously seek cover at all times. Their movements are not particularly quick or wiry. For a child's first snake this is the best.

As a variation in diet, try slugs and insect larvae, such as mealworms and smooth caterpillars. Brownsnakes eat these under natural conditions. Since these snakes are small and common, they can usually be obtained with little if any delay from the large snake dealers. They are among the most reasonably priced.

The LINESNAKE (*Tropidoclonion*) is only slightly larger than the Brownsnake, averaging about 12 inches and reaching a maximum of about 21 inches. The back is gray-brown with three well-defined light stripes, the belly whitish with two rows of round black spots. These snakes, like the Brownsnakes, virtually never bite. Their natural diet is almost exclusively earthworms. Sometimes specimens are reluctant to eat and must be force-fed. Once the initial reluctance is broken, the snakes eat eagerly. They are perhaps a little more attractive in appearance, in their slightly larger size, than the Brownsnakes, but the two are alike in their temperament. The Brownsnakes are much more easily obtained and less inclined toward self-starvation. The Linesnake occurs only in the Midwest, whereas the Brownsnakes occur over the entire eastern area and are much more easily obtained from dealers.

Young GARTERSNAKES and RIBBONSNAKES (*Thamnophis*) of most species (there are 13 in this country) eagerly eat earthworms. These are striped snakes (most species with bright stripes), and at small sizes (up to 15 inches) they are usually docile. At larger sizes (they reach three and one-half feet), fresh specimens are usually nervous and may strike repeatedly until accustomed to human presence. Although they are not difficult to tame, large specimens are not desirable for a beginner. If a small specimen is kept as a pet, however, and matures, the likelihood of its biting is remote, for the familiarity with humans learned early in life is not lost with increasing age and size.

Because even the young snakes are sometimes nervous enough to bite, although the bite can scarcely be felt, Gartersnakes are not as desirable as those previously mentioned. However, as snakes of country-wide occurrence they are cheaper than many others and can be found readily in most areas by your own search. Actually their food is highly varied, consisting of fish, leeches, slugs, frogs, toads, and salamanders. A few spe-

Two of the twelve subspecies of the widely distributed Ringneck snake (*Diadophis punctatus*) occurring in the United States. Above, the northern subspecies, *Diadophis punctatus edwardsi;* below, the western Regal subspecies, *Diadophis punctatus regalis.* The northern subspecies has few or no dots on its underside. When first disturbed, all Ringnecks tightly curl the tail and turn its bright red underside up.

Chionactis palarostris palarostris, the Sonoran Shovelnose snake, perhaps the most colorful of all North American snakes. An invertebrate eater, this snake is very docile but difficult to keep in captivity.

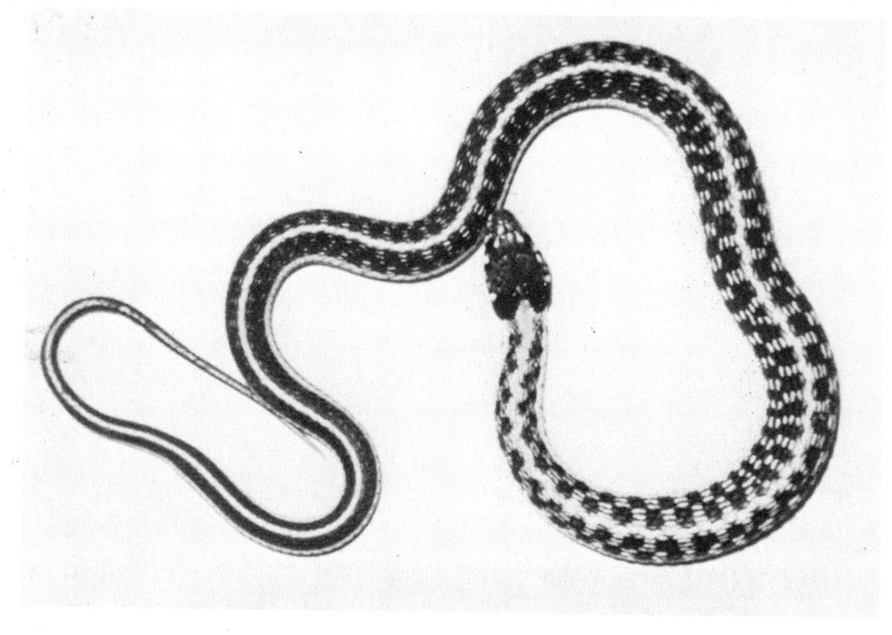

Figure 41a. The Black-necked Gartersnake, *Thamnophis cyrtopsis cyrtopsis.* The pair of large black blotches on the nape is distinctive.

Figure 41b. The midwest species of the Common Gartersnake, *Thamnophis sirtalis parietalis*; like all other western subspecies, it is red-barred.

cies eat mice and lizards. These are diet specializations more characteristic of adults, however; almost all young Gartersnakes will eat earthworms.

Barbara Froom has been eminently successful in keeping Gartersnakes as pets. Her account, as given in *The Young Naturalist*, a Canadian journal, follows:

"If you are considering a snake for a pet, a gartersnake is a good choice. It is common, hardy and eats a reasonable variety of foods. A young snake under 16 inches will adapt well to captivity.

"Before obtaining your snake, you would be wise to read about these fascinating creatures and how they differ from other pets. Also, their home in captivity should be prepared in advance.

"Snakes are excellent 'escape artists' and are best kept in a screen-topped terrarium. A medium-sized fish

Figure 41c. A Western Ribbonsnake, *Thamnophis proximus,* of the Gartersnake group. There is an Eastern Ribbonsnake, too, but it has a dark line along the edges of the ventrals. The Ribbonsnakes have a comparatively longer tail—over a quarter of their entire length—than the other Gartersnakes.

Two kinds of Ratsnake (*Elaphe*); above, the Lyre Ratsnake, *Elaphe guttata guttata,* the eastern and most colorful subspecies; below, the eastern Gulf subspecies (*Elaphe obsoleta spiloides*) of the Common Ratsnake. All Ratsnakes are constrictors and are readily kept as pets. The Common Ratsnake is less tractable than the other species.

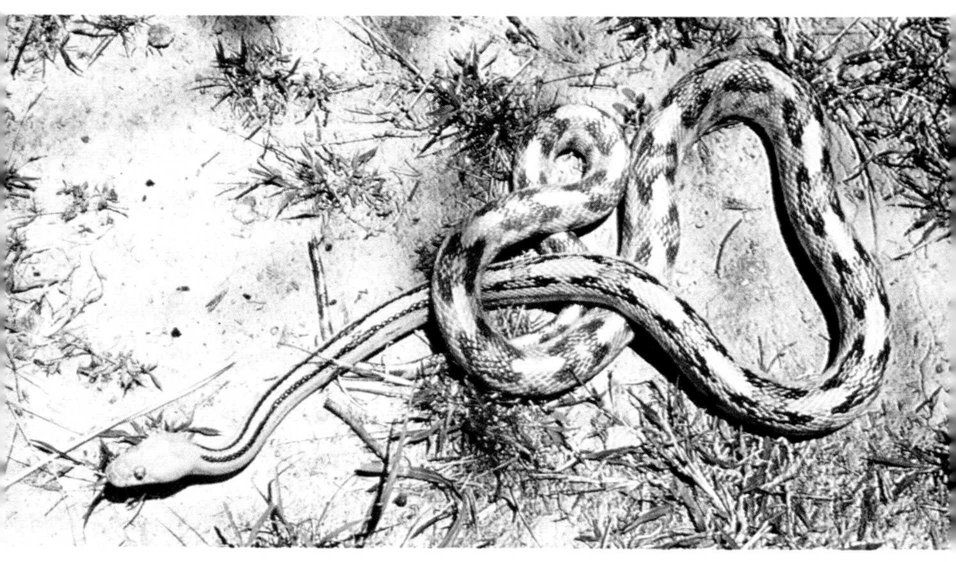

Two large and colorful western Ratsnake species, both of which are docile and highly prized: above, the Trans-Pecos Ratsnake (*Elaphe subocularis*); below, the Green Ratsnake (*Elaphe triaspis intermedia*). Note the large eye of the Trans-Pecos and the small bead-like scales of the Green.

tank fitted with a latched screen top would serve the purpose. With a little more difficulty, a 'snake pit' could also be made with panes of glass about 15 inches high. The sides of the glass should be taped and inserted with plaster of Paris into a bake pan. A plant in a small planter (with no holes in it), clean, dry sand in the bottom of the pan, a few colorful rocks and some driftwood will make an attractive, natural-appearing home for your pet. There must always be fresh water—a heavy glass ash tray will serve the purpose. Care must be taken to keep the surroundings dry. That is why the plant should be in a separate container, so that when it is watered the rest of the snake's home won't become damp and cause him to develop skin fungus. A little cardboard hut or hollow log is also appreciated by captive snakes. Snakes love to bask in the sun or in the light of a lamp, but they must not become overheated—there should always be a shady area.

"Most gartersnakes relish earthworms, which may be kept throughout the winter in earth in a cool place. In using worms, be sure only the large dew worms or common earthworms are used. The small red manure-bred worms are toxic to snakes, as are pickerel frogs, easily identified by the orange coloring on the underside of the legs. They also enjoy minnows and will learn to accept strips of raw fish and even raw beef and liver, especially if mixed with fish. When they are warm, gartersnakes may eat every second day. They will not hibernate if kept at house temperature. If your snake does not eat for two weeks after capture, it should be released.

"A small gartersnake usually does not attempt to bite, but when first captured it will lash about and release a scent. In eagerness for food, your pet might accidentally bite if it is hand-fed, thus it would be best to put its food on a small dish. Live minnows and worms

Figure 41d. Sand or fine gravel makes a good covering for the bottom of the cage of a pet snake like this Gartersnake, but the sand or gravel must be kept dry.

could be dropped into the water dish. See that the food does not become sand-coated. Minnows don't live long after they are obtained, but the dead ones can be put in the deep freeze, then thawed and fed as required. Sometimes snakes will refuse food if it is not alive, and this is one of the many difficulties encountered in keeping these reptiles. Remember, the snake's forked tongue is harmless and helps it to smell its food.

"Prior to skin shedding, the snake's eyes will become cloudy, and he will refuse food and appear listless. However, a few days after the eyes have cleared, you will see him literally "crawl out of his skin.' He will then be very eager for food. If you measure each skin, you will get some idea how much your pet has grown. Shed skin is transparent, lacking the coloration of the snake.

"With good care, gartersnakes may live for ten years or more in captivity."

The Speckled Racer, *Drymobius margaritiferus.* The illustrated subspecies is *Drymobius margaritiferus occidentalis,* from Chiapas, Mexico. In dorsal pattern this subspecies is scarcely distinguishable from the subspecies in the United States, *Drymobius margaritiferus margaritiferus.* The Speckled Racer accepts a wide range of foods but is not a particularly desirable pet.

Green Vinesnake, *Oxybelis fulgidus,* and Brown Vinesnake, *Oxybelis aeneus.* The Brown Vinesnake occurs in Arizona to South America; the Green Vinesnake occurs from southern Mexico to Argentina; they are both mildly poisonous, elongate species subsisting mostly on lizards.

Northern Watersnake, *Natrix sipedon sipedon*; this very common snake is easy to feed (fish, frogs) but is nasty-tempered and does not make a good pet.

The prettiest of all the worm-eating snakes are the WORMSNAKES (*Carphophis*, one species). They are a uniform black or brown above, pink below, and average about nine inches in length (13 maximum). Their chief handicaps as pets are their need for moisture and shade (requiring a terrarium instead of an ordinary cage), and their wiriness. They never bite, having a small, flat, pointed head and mouth, but when held constantly squirm and struggle, and thus seem not to respond to handling as well as the preceding groups. Moreover, they are not easy to feed, at least in my experience. Some owners state that they do well feeding on smooth caterpillars and other soft insect larvae, as well as earthworms. A secretive, nocturnal snake, this species is not often available from dealers. Its small size, however, means a low price.

The CONENOSE SNAKES (*Virginia*), of two very similar species, are nondescript, gray or brown animals above, and white to light pink below. They are small (average nine inches, maximum about 12) and moderately easy to tame. Like the Wormsnakes, they are virtually incapable of biting humans. Their diet is more varied, consisting of sowbugs, ants, insect larvae of various sorts, and even small lizards, as well as the staple earthworms. These species likewise are not commonly available, but make satisfactory and safe, if not spectacular, pets.

For the sake of completeness, I should mention one species of Watersnake—KIRTLAND'S WATERSNAKE (*Clonophis kirtlandi*), which lives almost exclusively upon earthworms and slugs. It makes an ideal pet, refusing to bite humans, and responding well to handling. It has a bright pattern and is larger than the previously mentioned species (average 15, maximum about 24 inches). Unfortunately, it is so restricted in distribution (Illinois to New Jersey) that dealers can seldom supply it alive, and even residents of this area find it rarely. A pair I once kept fed avidly on earthworms, exhibiting a strange ability to convince the worms that their mouths were but a refuge, into which the worms quickly and willingly crawled, and without further effort on the part of the snakes!

Perhaps we should include with the worm eaters the pretty little RINGNECK snakes (*Diadophis*). These are small (average 12 inches or so, maximum about two and one-half feet), completely docile snakes that can be relied upon never to bite. They are black above, usually with a yellow ring around the neck and red to yellow below with usually scattered black specks (see Fig. 42). Their only offensive habit is secreting a strong-smelling fluid from the anal scent glands, coiling the tail at the same time in a tight spiral with the brightly colored

Figure 42a. Ringneck snake; this is the subspecies *Diadophis punctatus edwardsi*.

Two color phases of the Banded Watersnake, *Natrix fasciata,* as exemplified by the Mangrove subspecies (*Natrix fasciata compressicauda*), which is largely restricted to salt and brackish waters of southern Florida. This subspecies is extremely variable in pattern and coloration; the tail base is slightly compressed.

The Coachwhip, *Masticophis flagellum,* as represented by the Great Plains subspecies (*Masticophis flagellum testaceus*). This specimen (from Colorado) exemplifies the reddish phase, but the red color is sometimes considerably brighter.

Figure 42b. *Diadophis punctatus regalis,* the largest subspecies of Ringneck snake.

under-surface turned up. This exposure is thought to be a protective device to frighten potential enemies away. Fortunately, the snakes very quickly cease to secrete the scent in captivity. Care must be taken to prevent these snakes from drying out; a fairly moist terrarium is desirable, although not essential. The biggest difficulty is getting them to eat. Actually they are omnivorous, eating almost any land animal small enough to swallow and large enough to grasp in their jaws. This, however, makes them no easier to feed. The diet includes smaller snakes, lizards, frogs, toads, salamanders, earthworms, insects, insect larvae and no doubt spiders, millipedes, and the like. Despite the difficulty of feeding, these snakes make very interesting, colorful and safe pets.

Other at least occasional earthworm eaters are the FLATHEAD SNAKES (*Tantilla*). They are light tan above, with (save one species) a dark head, and sometimes a light neck ring; the belly is pink to yellow. Their length averages eight to 10 inches, maximum about 14 inches. They can be relied upon not to bite. Like the Ringneck snakes, their food is extremely varied.

The Insect Eaters

This is the second most desirable group for beginners. Actually all are hard to feed, requiring busy hands to search out the insect food they may require. But they are completely safe, and some are colorful. All types of common invertebrates, even earthworms, should be fed them until the most acceptable is discovered. Crickets, grasshoppers, mealworms, cockroaches, sowbugs, small beetles, spiders, millipedes, caterpillars, insects of all sorts (except true bugs) should be reasonably suitable food selections. Sometimes small frogs or tadpoles are taken.

Figure 43. Rough Greensnake, *Opheodrys aestivus.*

Striped Whipsnake, *Masticophis lateralis*; in the United States, the range of this snake is limited to California. Note the divided subcaudals and divided anal.

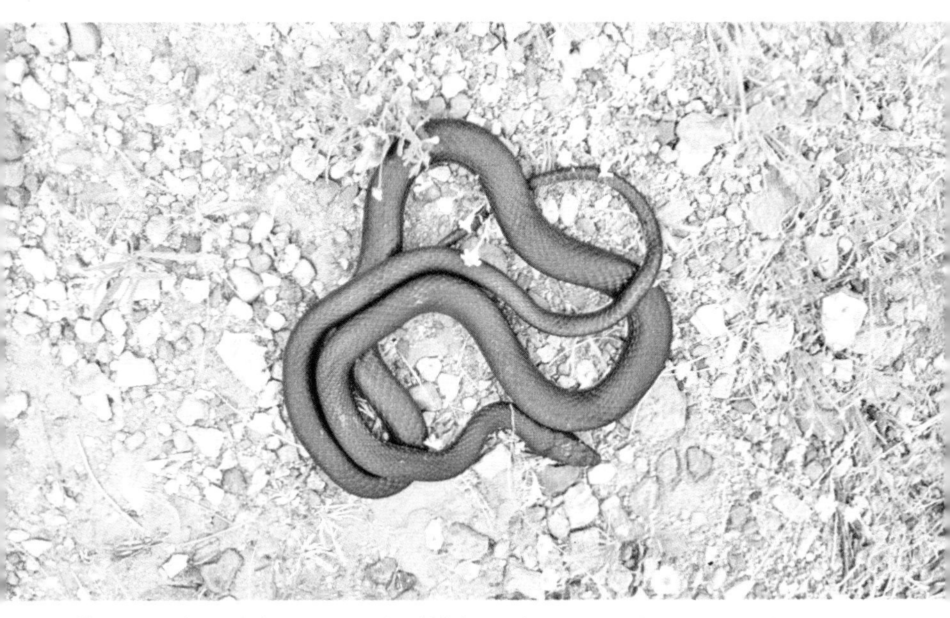

Two species of the aggressive Whipsnake group. Above, the Coachwhip (*Masticophis flagellum*), represented by the black phase of the western subspecies (*Masticophis flagellum piceus*). Below, the Lined Whipsnake, *Masticophis taeniatus taeniatus.*

Although challenging to feed, youngsters can often manage without difficulty. Searching for food is itself educational. The life span of these snakes is likely to be short, especially if food cannot be provided in winter.

The best pets of this group are the two species (rough and smooth) of GREENSNAKES (*Opheodrys*) (Fig. 43). Both are very slender, grass-green in color above, greenish-white below. They reach about three and one-half feet and are commonly one and three-quarters to two feet in length. They almost never bite, and the bite when given is negligible. These species make pets of never-failing interest and are rather frequently available from dealers. For a good discussion of proper care of these snakes, see the account quoted from Froom in the preceding section on "Assist-Feeding." In some areas they readily eat daddy longlegs (harvestmen).

The GROUNDSNAKES (*Sonora*) are small, reliable snakes that never bite and eat fairly well. Their pattern is highly variable, but the general tone is a light tan above and light pink below, with or without one or more crossbands on the body. They are common in the Midwest and should be reasonably priced. Other small insect eaters are the BLINDSNAKES (*Leptotyphlops*), SANDSNAKES (*Chilomeniscus*), SHOVELNOSE SNAKE (*Chionactis*), SHARPTAIL SNAKE (*Contia*), and HOOKNOSE SNAKES (*Ficimia* and *Gyalopion*). All are relatively rare, but if available should make very interesting pets. None bites humans at any time.

The Fish Eaters

Quite a few species of snakes eat fish either regularly or as conditions permit, and can be kept in captivity chiefly on this diet. The advantage of fish is that they can be readily obtained at all times of the year, either fresh or frozen. Strips cut from the fish are usually just as acceptable as whole or live fish, for these snakes rely chiefly on odor to guide them to their food. Unfortunately, most of the fish eaters bite rather freely and are somewhat difficult to tame. Use of soft leather gloves is recommended when handling the snakes, at least until they are adjusted to the conditions of captivity. Even when well-tamed, snakes of this group tend to become excited when they smell food and may strike any moving objects, especially those carrying the odor. Thus it is well to keep the food away from gloves used for handling the snakes and to wash the hands thoroughly of food odors before reaching into the snakes' cage.

Small snakes of this group are not likely to give a painful bite, and all readily accept fish food. Larger specimens (between about 15 and 24 inches) can bite rather sharply, drawing blood from each tooth-prick. From snakes larger than 24 inches the bite is often painful and severe. All bites drawing blood should, of course, be given antiseptic treatment, but seldom is anything further necessary, unless the part is jerked while bitten. In such cases the teeth pull through the flesh, making shallow cuts that may require adhesive bandages for protection.

Another unpleasant habit of the fish eaters is releasing small quantities of evil-smelling secretion from a pair of anal scent glands. Sometimes this is mixed with the suddenly freed watery contents of the rectum. The snake usually thrashes about in the process, scattering the repulsive mixture far and wide. Fortunately, snakes stop this after becoming accustomed to captivity, although even at best one never knows when the rectum may be emptied suddenly.

In spite of these dangers, the snakes of this group *can* be tamed to a wholly satisfactory degree. I have had many pets belonging to this group, as have others.

The most tractable and readily available are the

Masticophis taeniatus taeniatus, the Lined Whipsnake, from a Colorado specimen. (This is a younger individual than the snake of the same species illustrated on page 125.) The young have fewer fine lines down the scalerows than the older specimens do.

Carphophis amoenus amoenus, the eastern subspecies of the diminutive Wormsnake, a burrower. This worm- and insect-eating species is docile but difficult to keep in captivity.

GARTERSNAKES (*Thamnophis*), most species of which will accept fish at all stages of growth. Exceptions seem to be the Ribbon Gartersnakes (*T. sauritus*, *T. proximus*) and certain terrestrial races of the Western Gartersnake (*T. elegans*). All are striped snakes, reaching a length of three and one-half feet, averaging 20 inches or more. They become tame fairly easily. Their bite is not generally as severe as in the Watersnakes. A wide variety of food is taken by the Gartersnakes, and for a change in diet they may be offered any animal small enough to swallow. They are known to eat insects and insect larvae, birds, mice, salamanders, frogs, toads and lizards. In view of the rather fixed racial and individual preferences that exist, it is sometimes necessary to experiment if fish are not readily taken.

Another group of fish eaters is the WATERSNAKES (*Natrix*, Fig. 44) excluding, however, the dwarf species (see earthworm and crayfish eaters). These snakes reach a large size (maximum of five and one-half feet), some being among the most vicious nonvenomous snakes of the country. A big Watersnake seldom makes a good pet, simply because of its unpredictable viciousness and the extensive laceration its bite may cause. Smaller specimens are less dangerous, but little different in temperament. These snakes may appear stupid, and in many ways they are. But even such confirmed rascals quickly learn if their bites do not ward off supposed enemies. In this respect, gloves may be very useful in teaching them the futility of biting.

It is unfortunate that Watersnakes are so irascible, for they include some truly beautifully marked species (for instance, the southern race, *confluens*, of the Banded Watersnake). The experienced snake fancier willing to use patience with novel species is well rewarded for his extra effort by the beauty of some of his pets. The most beautiful are several races of the Banded

Figure 44. Common Watersnake, *Natrix sipedon sipedon;* see also pages 117, 120 and Figure 14 for other illustrations of Watersnakes.

Watersnake. Next most desirable are the other races of the Common Watersnake, especially the southern ones. The Green, Brown and Diamond-back Watersnakes are rather nondescript, very large and least desirable as pets. The Brazos Watersnake may be desirable, since it is small and in some specimens is delicately shaded, but it is rare. All these species are rabid fish eaters, but accept frogs, toads, tadpoles, salamanders and young turtles.

Another species of fish eater is the small BLACK SWAMPSNAKE (*Seminatrix*). This is a rather docile species, biting only occasionally. It is black above and pink below, with black cross-bars. If it were not so rare, it would be highly recommended as a pet species.

The Toad and Frog Eaters

Included in this group are some snakes that eat almost nothing but toads, and a few others that eat frogs and lizards, and sometimes even small mice. Actually, most Watersnakes and Gartersnakes accept toads and frogs, but ordinarily this food does not play an important role in captivity, because it is difficult to obtain. If a supply is available, other snakes in addition to members of this group may, of course, profit from it, but the best course is to feed the toads to the more specialized species listed below.

The HOGNOSE SNAKES (*Heterodon*) are the most interesting of all. They are fat and short; surprisingly enough, despite initial indication, they never bite.

Figure 45. Eastern Hognose snake, *Heterodon platyrhinos.* See also Figures 5, 15, 16 and pages 57 and 60 for other illustrations of Hognose snakes.

These are the spreading, puffing, native snakes (often called "adders," "puff adders," or "spreading adders") that stage such a showy bluff of being fierce, but are actually as gentle as kittens. The bluffing performance is followed by an attempt to play dead, the snakes turning on the back, with the mouth open and tongue dangling out. They refuse to perform, however, after a few days in captivity, becoming the most docile of all snakes.

Averaging perhaps 18 to 20 inches in length, with a rather heavy body, this snake makes a showy, tractable pet. Its food consists almost wholly of toads, to which these snakes are highly adapted. Frogs are sometimes eaten in captivity, and rarely birds. Insects also may be eaten.

The SLENDER SNAKE (*Rhadinaea*) is a rare, docile species of brownish color, seldom offered for sale. It eats frogs, toads and lizards more or less indiscriminately.

The CATEYE SNAKE (*Leptodeira*) is another rare but not very docile species, with broad brown blotches on the light ground color of the back. Its food habits resemble those of the Slender Snake.

For lack of a better place we include here two spectacular, large, pretty and docile snakes which are hard to feed in captivity. The MUDSNAKES (*Farancia*) feed normally upon large aquatic salamanders, but these are seldom available for captives. Frogs, toads and fish may be substituted. These snakes are truly marvelous pets for show and tractability, despite the difficulty in feeding. The Checkered Mudsnakes are a glossy black above, and checkered black and red on the sides and belly. They reach a length of six feet. The Rainbow Mudsnake is shiny, striped with black and red above, pinkish-yellow on the sides, and salmon-red speckled with black below. It reaches a length of about five feet.

Probably the snakes in this group are more commonly used as pets than any others. Certain ones are relatively safe pets, seldom biting. They are large and often attractively marked; they adjust well in every way to life in captivity. I have not placed them at the top of the order of preference simply because they are relatively large, and all *can* bite. A child should not start with any snake of this group measuring more than one and one-half feet, because of the relative severity of a possible bite, even if it is only a small one. An exception should be made only if an experienced adult can actively supervise the handling of the snake at least until its temperament is known. Once the snake is adjusted to handling, the chance of a bite is remote. If proper care is taught the child, the chance is negligible. For more experienced handlers, the snakes of this group are ideal.

A further difficulty of keeping these snakes is obtaining adequate food. Wild mice and sparrows may be trapped, but usually sources for such animals are promptly exhausted. White mice, rats or hamsters may be purchased from various supply houses, but this becomes expensive. A breeding stock may be established. It requires considerable space and is usually odorous. Baby chicks, especially rejects, are an economical and convenient food for snakes of moderate and large size. Local colleges or hospitals sometimes can spare excess experimental or test animals.

Most snakes—and this group is no exception—require their food alive, although they occasionally find and eat carcasses of animals that have died from various causes. Once the snakes are adjusted to captivity, they may be led to accept freshly-killed food. Seldom will they take cold, dead prey. Movements rather than odor dominate these snakes' recognition of food. It is possible that artificially warmed food animals, previously either frozen or merely kept cool, may be acceptable to them.

The Mouse Eaters

The most attractive snake pets, although not the safest so far as biting is concerned, are the mouse eaters. Actually, these snakes accept all kinds of small mammals they can swallow, from shrews to young rabbits. Almost all will accept small birds, at least in captivity. Others will feed on various animals, as circumstances permit.

The chief characteristic of the mouse-eater diet is that it consists of warm blooded animals. Snakes wholly or largely reliant on this sort of diet are constrictors, killing their prey by squeezing hard enough to stop breathing. The others, more nearly omnivorous, do not constrict, but simply hold their prey down with a loop of the body, or with the mouth. Sometimes they start to swallow it before it is dead. The non-constrictors cannot, of course, readily subdue the larger mammals, like rats and gophers, which the constrictors handle easily.

Figure 46. Northern Rosy Boa, *Lichanura trivirgata roseofusca.* See also page 33.

There are two native BOAS (*Lichanura, Charina*) in this country. Both are small as Boas go (one and one-half to three feet), but are as safe as any snake can be. So far as I am aware, they never bite humans. They are extremely quiet, slow-moving, never exhibiting the nervous actions almost all other snakes possess to some degree. If it were not for the difficulty in securing food for them, these would be the best of all snake pets. The Rosy Boa (*Lichanura*) is a striped snake; the Rubber Boa (*Charina*) is a uniform gray or gray-brown, known to eat lizards occasionally in the wild.

The KINGSNAKES (*Lampropeltis*) are the next best pets. Occasionally they may offer to bite at first, but after a very brief period of captivity they become completely docile. Some forms reach nearly six feet; most are about two to three feet in length. Color and pattern differ greatly in the six species of this country. Most common pets are the various races of the Speckled Kingsnake, the Yellowbellied Kingsnake, and the Eastern Red Kingsnake. Of the last, specimens from the Southwest and Midwest (not eastern ones) are prettily

Figure 47. *Lampropeltis triangulum amaura,* the Western Gulf subspecies of the Eastern Red Kingsnake.

Figure 48. *Lampropeltis zonata multicincta,* the more eastern subspecies of the Sierra Red Kingsnake.

Figure 49. *Lampropeltis zonata multicincta;* compare with Figure 48 for variation. The species is limited to California, ranging perhaps as far north as Washington.

Figure 50. *Lampropeltis calligaster calligaster,* the Yellowbellied Kingsnake, an excellent pet species, docile and easily fed.

Figure 51. *Lampropeltis triangulum gentilis,* the Central Plains subspecies of the Eastern Red Kingsnake.

Figure 52. *Lampropeltis triangulum triangulum,* the eastern subspecies of the Eastern Red Kingsnake.

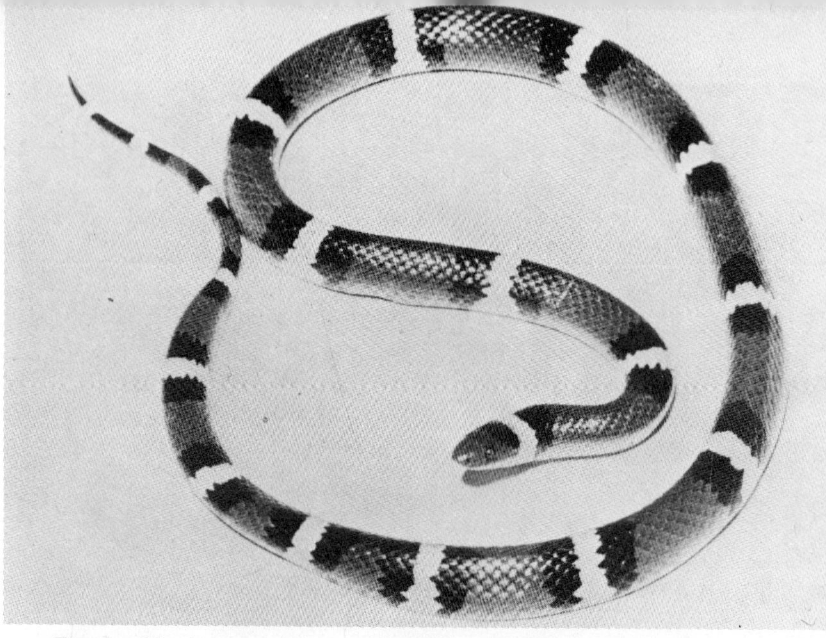

Figure 53. *Lampropeltis triangulum elapsoides,* the Scarlet subspecies of the Eastern Red Kingsnake. Occurring within the range of the venomous Coralsnake, this snake is often confused with the latter. The belly usually is not completely ringed in the Scarlet Kingsnake, and the red is bordered by black, whereas in the Coralsnake the rings always encircle the belly and the red is bordered by yellow.

marked with red. Also attractively marked with red are the two species of Western Red Kingsnakes. The other species is very rare.

Kingsnakes eat almost anything, even insects. They are especially well known for their "cannibalism." They eat almost any smaller snakes, even Rattlesnakes, Copperheads, and other poisonous species, to whose venom Kingsnakes are partially immune. Not all species (or individuals) will accept snakes, however, or any other single food item. Experiments may be necessary to determine what is acceptable. Other food items recorded are lizards, fishes, eggs of turtles and birds, frogs, salamanders, and slugs.

Next in order of preference are the BULLSNAKES (*Pituophis*). They reach a very large size (nearly eight

Figure 54. Central Plains Bullsnake, *Pituophis melanoleucus sayi*. See pages 36 and 37 for additional illustrations of Bullsnakes.

feet). Like the Kingsnakes, they may be a little nervous at first, but very quickly become completely docile and make very reliable, safe pets. All are yellow and brownish, blotched or speckled. When frightened they part their jaws slightly and hiss loudly. Their food is almost exclusively small mammals, with occasional birds.

The INDIGO SNAKE (*Drymarchon*) is also popular as a pet. It is a sleek bluish-black or mixture of black and brown, often with a little reddish color on the belly. The body is fairly heavy, reaching a length of eight or more feet. Like Bullsnakes the Indigo snake usually becomes docile after a brief period in captivity. However, some individuals remain unpredictably prone to bite, and the bite from such a large snake is not a passing matter. Nevertheless this is the popular side-show carnival pet, often used in feminine "snake-charmer" roles.

Some RATSNAKES (*Elaphe*), especially the Lyre Ratsnake (*Elaphe guttata guttata*, Fig. 56) make good pets. The eastern phase of the latter species is especially beautifully marked with red spots. The Fox Ratsnake (*Elaphe vulpina*, Fig. 57) is almost equally docile. It is attractively blotched with brown on a speckled yellow and brown background. Other species (Common and Green Ratsnakes) are, more often than not, irascible for life, biting freely even after years in captivity. The numerous color races of the Common Ratsnake include the so-called Pilot Blacksnake, Chickensnake (Fig. 58),

Figure 55. Indigo snake, *Drymarchon corais*.

Figure 56. Lyre Ratsnake, *Elaphe guttata guttata,* the eastern "Cornsnake" subspecies. See other illustrations of Ratsnakes in Figures 33, 35, 57, 58, 59 and on pages 112 and 113.

Striped Ratsnake or Yellow Ratsnake (Figs. 33, 35), and others.

Size averages from two to three feet for all members of the genus, maximum being about six to eight

Figure 57. Fox Ratsnake, *Elaphe vulpina,* one of the most docile of the Ratsnakes. This is an excellent pet species that often has been bred through several generations in captivity.

Figure 58. Common Ratsnake, *Elaphe obsoleta lindheimeri,* exemplified by the Western Gulf, or Chickensnake, subspecies. It does very well in captivity but is too feisty to be prized as a pet species.

Figure 59. *Elaphe obsoleta obsoleta,* the northern subspecies (often called "Pilot Blacksnake" or "Black Ratsnake") of the Common Ratsnake. This is the only subspecies of *Elaphe obsoleta* that tends to become nearly uniformly black in large adults.

Figure 60. *Coluber constrictor flaviventris,* the midwestern Blue Racer.

feet. Although their food consists chiefly of small mammals, this group more than any other indulges in small birds and eggs; rarely are snakes, lizards or frogs taken.

The RACERS (*Coluber* and *Drymobius*) and WHIPSNAKES (*Masticophis*) are fast-moving, nervous snakes of a vicious temperament, seldom quieted. Contrary to most others, these snakes bite tenaciously, chewing for several seconds after grasping an object in

Figure 61. *Masticophis flagellum flagellum,* the eastern subspecies of the Coachwhip. This is the largest of the seven subspecies found in the United States; adults are black anteriorly, brown posteriorly on their upper surfaces.

their jaws. They are not especially desirable pets. The so-called "Blacksnake," "Blue Racer" (Fig. 60), and "Black Racer" (Figs. 32, 34) are color phases of the true Racers (*Coluber*). The Speckled Racer (*Drymobius*) is a speckled yellow-on-black species of southern Texas. The Coachwhip (Fig. 61) is a close relative of the Whip-snakes, belonging in the same genus. All are rather completely omnivorous, eating mammals, birds, snakes, lizards, amphibians and insects.

The Lizard Eaters

With completion of the mouse-eating group, the best pets have been described. There remain a few other western snakes, mostly rare, that live on a diet chiefly of lizards or snakes. None are particularly desirable as pets, but all are fairly tractable and can readily be tamed. Among those whose main diet is lizards are the LEAFNOSE SNAKES (*Phyllorhynchus*), with a most grotesquely enlarged snout plate; PATCHNOSE SNAKES (*Salvadora*), with a less enlarged snout plate;

Figure 62. *Arizona elegans occidentalis,* the California subspecies of the Glossy snake. See page 53 for illustration of another Glossy snake subspecies.

LONGNOSE SNAKES (*Rhinocheilus*), with considerable red in the speckled ground color surrounding brownish blotches; GLOSSY SNAKES (*Arizona*), looking like gray Bullsnakes; NIGHTSNAKES (*Hypsiglena*), small blotched snakes of nocturnal habits; COFFEE-SNAKES (*Coniophanes*), with broad brown stripes; VINESNAKES (*Oxybelis*) of very slender, elongate build; and LYRESNAKES (*Trimorphodon*), with slight venomous properties.

The Snake Eaters

The beautifully marked red-blotched SCARLET-SNAKE (*Cemophora*), and the gray or brown-blotched SHORTTAIL SNAKE (*Stilosoma*), both small, southeastern species of one and one-half feet, are almost exclusively snake-eaters. They are very docile, but difficult to feed in captivity, unless a supply of small snakes is available.

Figure 63. *Salvadora hexalepis hexalepis,* the eastern "Desert" subspecies of the Western Patchnose snake, centering in Arizona. Two other subspecies occur in the United States, one in coastal California and one northward into Nevada.

Figure 64. *Cemophora coccinea coccinea,* the Florida subspecies of the Scarlet snake. This is a doubly confusable species, resembling the Eastern Red Kingsnake as well as the venomous Coralsnake. Unlike the two species with which it is confused, however, the Scarlet snake has an unmarked belly, and it is easily separated from the Coralsnakes, which have their red rings bordered by yellow instead of black.

The Crayfish Eaters

Lastly comes a group almost wholly addicted to a diet of crayfish. All are small (one and one-half feet), feebly striped and as a rule gentle-mannered. The STRIPED SWAMPSNAKE (*Liodytes*) and three species of CRAYFISH SNAKES (*Regina grahami, R. rigida, R. septemvittata*), also striped, comprise this group.

11. Other Sources of Information

For further information on the natural history of snakes, see Pope's *Snakes Alive* and Curran and Kauffeld's *Snakes and Their Ways*. These excellent accounts make easy yet stimulating reading. Morris' *Boy's Book of Snakes* is informative and much liked. Other books specifically about snakes are the two by Parker, of worldwide scope; Shaw and Campbell's *Snakes of the American West;* and Kauffeld's *Snakes: The Keeper and the Kept*, perhaps the best book ever written on the care of snakes. Oliver's *Natural History of North American Amphibians and Reptiles,* written from the ecological point of view, contains much data on snakes and an excellent, brief discussion on keeping all kinds of reptiles and amphibians in captivity. Pope's *Reptile World* treats snakes and other reptiles, with emphasis on the North American species. Neill's excellent *Reptiles and Amphibians in the Service of Man* should be considered required general reading, even though it concerns more than snakes. Authoritative texts in the broad subject of herpetology are Goin and Goin's *Introduction to Herpetology* and Porter's *Herpetology*.

The best guide to identification of eastern snakes is Conant's most recent *Field Guide;* the equivalent for western snakes is Stebbins' *Field Guide*, although its scientific names are not completely up-to-date. Even less recent but still useful for detail are Wright and

Wright's *Handbook of Snakes* and Schmidt and Davis' *Field Book of Snakes.*

The barest essentials for snake identification—the key accompanied by statements of range for each species—are found in Perkins' *Key to the Snakes of the United States.* It, too, is somewhat dated as to scientific names, but it is cheap, accurate, condensed and handy.

Stebbins' *Amphibians and Reptiles of Western North America* provides more detail than his more recent *Field Guide*, and is therefore highly valuable as a supplementary reference. Shaw and Campbell's *Snakes of the American West* provides a more recent nomenclature and may be useful in identification. Embracing the entire country are Cochran and Goin's *The New Field Book* and Leviton's *Reptiles and Amphibians of North America.*

Some other sources are listed in the "References" at the end of this book. A large number of children's books on snakes have been published in recent years. Book dealers and public libraries will be glad to aid in finding any number as desired.

Anyone interested in amphibians or in snakes and other reptiles may subscribe to any of the several journals published on the subject. There are many amateur organizations, most of which publish a newsletter, bulletin or other periodical. These societies are so widely scattered over the country that at least one is almost certain to be nearby, regardless of locality. Unfortunately there is a considerable turnover among the organizations; local colleges may be able to provide guidance to the nearest. Lists of them appear from time to time in *Herpetological Review.*

There are three leading professional journals published in North America, all obtainable by anyone interested. *Herpetologica,* the journal of the Herpetologists' League, is issued four times a year (about 300 pages) and includes many articles on amphibians and reptiles throughout the world. The *Journal of Herpetology*, published by the Society for the Study of Amphibians and Reptiles, is the most recent and most active of the American journals in this field; the society sponsors a highly authoritative loose-leaf (presently incomplete but continually augmented) *Checklist* of rigorously thorough detail, as well as a more popular journal, the *Herpetological Review*. *Copeia*, the journal of the American Society of Ichthyologists and Herpetologists, is the oldest of the three and is published quarterly (about 150-250 pages each issue); it includes about as many papers annually in herpetology (even though about half of the journal is devoted to ichthyology) as the other journals.

Information about any or all of these societies and journals may be obtained from the Curator, Division of Herpetology, University of Kansas, Lawrence, Kansas, 66045.

Many local and regional amateur herpetologists' societies exist in North America. Inquiry at the above address will help in location of those of greatest interest.

REFERENCES

ALLEN, E. ROSS, and WILFRED T. NEILL, 1950. *Keep them alive! How to keep snakes, lizards, turtles, alligators and crocodiles in captivity.* Ross Allen's Reptile Institute, Special Publication No. 1, Silver Springs, Florida, 24 pp.

AYMAR, BRANDT, 1956. *Treasury of snake lore.* Greenberg, N.Y. An excellent review of snakes in general literature. 400 pp.

BARKER, WILL, 1964. *Familiar reptiles and Amphibians of America.* Harper & Row, New York. xix, 220 pp. (partly color). (Medium level, not especially authoritative.)

BELLAIRS, ANGUS D'A, 1958. *Reptiles.* 2nd Ed., Hutchinson's Univ. Library, London. 195 pp., 12 figs. Harper Torchbook, 1960. An excellent, scholarly account of classification, anatomy and habits of all reptiles, group by group.

—1969. *The life of reptiles.* Weidenfeld and Nicolson, London. 2 vols. (Textbook level, covering world and all reptiles.)

and RICHARD CARRINGTON, 1966. *The world of reptiles.* Chatto and Windus, London. 153 pp., 26 figs., 16 pls. (Semi-popular, world coverage, all reptiles, authoritative.)

BREEN, JOHN F., 1974. *Encyclopedia of reptiles and amphibians.* T.F.H. Publications, Inc. P.O. Box 27, Neptune, N.J. 07753. 576 pp., ill. (partly in color). (Medium level, worldwide coverage.)

BROWN, VINSON, 1974. *Reptiles and amphibians of the west.* Naturegraph, Healdsburg, Calif. 79 pp., ill. (partly color). (Western North America, largely identification, color weak.)

BUREAU OF SPORT FISHERIES AND WILDLIFE (Washington, D.C.), 1962a. *Earthworms for bait.* U.S. Dept. Interior, Fish and Wildlife Service, Leaflet FL-23: 1-5 (Detailed directions for collecting, raising, storing, harvesting, control and marketing.)

—1962b. *Fish baits: their collection, care, preparation, and propagation.* U.S. Dept. Interior, Fish and Wildlife Service, Leaflet FL-28: 1-25. (Numerous foods acceptable to snakes are discussed: earthworms, crickets, roaches, mealworms, frogs, salamanders, catalpa worms, minnows and mice.)

BURTON, MAURICE, 1973. *The world of reptiles and amphibians.* Crown, New York. vi, 128 pp., ill. (color). (Popular, oversize pictures.)

—1975. *Encyclopedia of reptiles, amphibians and other cold-blooded animals.* Octopus, London. 252 pp., ill. (color). (Popular, oversized pictures.)

CARNOCHAN, F.G., and H.C. ADAMSON, 1935. *The empire of the snakes.* Frederick A. Stokes, New York, 290 pp., ill.

CARR, ARCHIE, 1963. *The reptiles.* Life Nature Library. Time, Inc., New York, 192 pp., ill (many in color). The best general account of reptiles every written.

COCHRAN, DORIS M. and COLEMAN J. GOIN, 1970. *The new field book of reptiles and amphibians.* Putnam's, New York. xx, 359 pp., 16 pls. (color), 100 figs. (Authoritative identification manual.)

CONANT, ROGER, 1971. "Reptile and Amphibian Management Practices at Philadelphia Zoo," *International Zoo Yearbook*, 11: 224-230.

—1972. *Reptile Study.* Boy Scouts of America, New York. 64 pp., ill. (Excellent manual of amphibian-reptile care.)

—1975. *A field guide to reptiles and amphibians of eastern and central North America.* Houghton Mifflin, Boston. xviii, 429 pp., 105 figs. 311 maps, 48 pls. (color). (The best identification manual for the area.)

CURRAN, C.H., and CARL KAUFFELD, 1937. *Snakes and their ways.* Harper Bros., New York. xvii, 285 pp., ill.

FICHTER, GEORGE, 1968. *Snakes and other reptiles.* Golden Press, New York. 80 pp., ill. (color). (low medium level, North American coverage.)

FITZSIMONS, F.W., 1932. *Snakes.* Hutchison, London. 286 pp., 44 figs. (Anecdotal recollections of a famed South African zoo herpetologist.)

FROOM, BARBARA, 1962. "The Smooth Green Snake (*Opheodrys vernalis*) in Captivity." Bull, Philadelphia Herpetological Soc., 10(1): 11-13.

—1972. *The Snakes of Canada.* McCelland & Stewart, Toronto. 128 pp., ill., 21 figs. in color. (Excellent, thorough, authoritative review.)

FRYE, FEDERIC L., 1973. *Husbandry, medicine and surgery in captive reptiles.* VM Publ. Co., Bonner Springs, Kansas. 140 pp., ill. (partly color). (The ultimate in reptilian care, by a practicing veterinarian with much experience.)

GANS, CARL, 1975. *Reptiles of the world.* Bantam, New York. 159 pp., ill. (color). (Small, extremely brief, authoritative.)

—1969-1973. *Biology of the Reptilia.* Academic Press, New York. Several vols. (continuing series). (Technical series, so far largely anatomical and physiological; reviews of limited, specific topics by numerous specialists.)

GLIDDEN, H. SPENCER, 1936. *Diseases of reptiles.* Florida Reptile Institute, Silver Springs, Florida, 7 pp.

GOIN, COLEMAN, J. and OLIVE B. GOIN, *Introduction to herpetology.* San Francisco; Freeman, xi, 353 pp. ill. (One of two formal textbooks of herpetology as a discipline; see also Porter.)

GRZIMEK, BERNHARD, HEINI HEDIGER, KONRAD KLEMMER, OSCAR KUHN and HEINZ WERMUTH, 1975. *Reptiles. In: Grzimek's animal life encyclopedia, Volume 6.* Van Nostrand Reinhold, New York. 589 pp., ill. (mostly color). (A definitely superior, authoritative manual of classification, distribution, diversity.)

HARMAN, IAN, 1950. *Reptiles as pets.* Blanford Press Ltd., London, W.C.I 115 pp. (11 pp. on snakes). European (especially British) emphasis.

HOKE, JOHN, 1952. *The first book of snakes.* Franklin Watts, Inc., 117 W. 57th St. New York 10019, 69 pp. (median grade school level.)

HOOPES, ISABEL, 1963. *Reptiles in the home zoo.* New England Museum of Natural History. Special Publication No. 1. 64 pp.

HOWEY, M. OLDFIELD, 1955. *The encircled serpent.* Arthur Richmond Co., New York. A thorough review of snake symbolism in the cultures of man. xi, 411 pp., ill.

HYLANDER, C.J., 1951. *Adventures with reptiles: The story of Ross Allen.* Messner, New York. xii, 174 pp., ill. (An account of the early life of an exhibit-oriented herpetologist of legendary fame in his field.)

JOHNSON, TOM R., ROBERT N. BADER and DONALD J. COXWELL, 1975. *Amphibians and reptiles in captivity.* St. Louis Herp. Society, Special issue, (2): i-iii, 1-35, ill. (Brief review through personal experiences of the authors of care of locally available herps of all kinds.)

KAUFFELD, CARL, 1957. *Snakes and snake hunting.* Hanover House, Garden City, N.Y. 266 pp., ill. An entertaining account of a snake-collector's life in the field.

—1969. *Snakes: the keeper and the kept.* Doubleday, Garden

City, N.Y. xiv, 248 pp., 39 fig. (Experiences and admonitions for care of snakes by one of the most knowledgeable of zoo men; accounts of field trips.)

KLAUBER, L.M., 1972. *Rattlesnakes; their habits, life histories and influence on mankind.* Second edition. Univ. Calif. Press, Berkeley, Calif. 2 vols. An exhaustive review.

KLINGELHOFFER, WILHELM, 1955-9. *Terrarienkunde.* Vols. 1-4. Alfred Kernen Verlag, Schloss-Strasse 80, Stuttgart, Germany. 1046 pp., 751 figs., 16 col. pls. The most complete book in existence on care of reptiles and amphibians in captivity. In German.

KUNDERT, F., 1974. *Fascination: snakes and lizards.* Kundert, Spreitenbach, Switzerland. 201 pp. ill. (mostly color). (The most striking photographs, mostly of snakes, ever published.)

LANE, MARGARET, 1963. *Life with Ionides.* Hamilton, London. ix, 180 pp., ill. (partly color). (A biography of a fugitive from civilization who devoted his life to collecting animals, especially snakes, in the wilds of Africa. See also Wykes.)

LUETSCHER, ALFRED, 1963. *A study of reptiles and amphibians, including their care as pets.* Blandford, London. 80 pp., 68 figs. (Sound, authoritative, but largely of European orientation.)

—1966. *A young specialist looks at reptiles and amphibians.* Burke, London. 148 pp. ill. (European orientation.)

MERTENS, ROBERT, 1960. *The world of amphibians and reptiles.* George G. Harrap, London. 207 pp., 16 pls. in color, 80 in black and white.

MINTON, SHERMAN A., JR., 1974. *Venom diseases.* C.C. Thomas, Springfield, Ill. xv, 235 pp., 62 figs. (A technically sound discourse on knowledge of venom action and treatment by a practicing physician famed in herpetology.)

and MADGE RUTHERFORD MINTON. *Venomous reptiles.* 1969. Scribner's, New York. xii, 274 pp., ill. (Semipopular, authoritative, worldwide coverage.)

MOORE, GRANVILLE M., SHERMAN A. MINTON, HERNDON G. DOWLING and FINDLAY E. RUSSELL, 1968. *Poisonous snakes of the world: a manual for use by U.S. amphibious forces.* U.S. Govt. Printing Office, Washington, D.C. viii, 212 pp., 120 figs., 8 col. pls. (The best in its field.)

MORRIS PERCY A., 1948. *Boy's book of snakes. How to recognize and understand them.* Ronald Press Co., 15 E. 26th St., New York. 85 pp.

—1974. *An introduction to the reptiles and amphibians of the United States.* Dover, New York. xii, 253 pp., ill., frontis. (Medium level.)

MORRIS, RAMONA and DESMOND MORRIS, 1965. *Men and snakes.* McGraw-Hill, New York. 224 pp., ill. (Cultural impact of snakes, worldwide coverage.)

MURPHY, JAMES B., 1975. *A brief outline of suggested treatments for diseases of captive reptiles.* Soc. Study Amph. Repts., Misc. Publ. Herp. Circular (4): i-ii 1-13. (Excellent, but painfully brief starter; good bibliography.)

NEILL, WILFRED T., 1974. *Reptiles and amphibians in the service of man.* Bobbs-Merril, Indianapolis, Ind. ix, 248 pp. 70 figs. (Splendid review of one of herpetology's rare geniuses.)

NOWINSKY, IRA, 1967. *Enjoy your snakes.* Pet Library, New York. 30 pp., ill. (mostly color). (Brief, popular.)

OLDHAM, JONATHAN C., HOBART M. SMITH and SUE ANN MILLER, 1970. *A laboratory perspectus of snake anatomy.* Stipes, Champaign, Illinois. v, 98 pp., ill. (The only readily available manual of snake anatomy; college level.)

OLIVER, JAMES A., 1955. *The natural history of North American amphibians and reptiles.* D. Van Nostrand Co., Inc., 120 Alexander St., Princeton, N.J. 359 pp.

—1958. *Snakes in fact and fiction.* Macmillan Co., New York. 200 pp., ill. An informative investigation of folklore, particularly on maximum sizes of the largest snakes.

PARKER, MALCOLM, 1963. *Snakes.* Hale, London. 191 pp., 11 figs. 16 pls. (A discourse by one of the former leading herpetologists of the world; worldwide scope.)

—1965. *Natural history of snakes.* British Museum (Natural History), London. v, 95 pp., 18 figs., 6 pls. (A condensation of the preceding.)

PERKINS, C.B., 1949. *A key to the snakes of the United States.* Zoological Society of San Diego, Calif., Bull. No. 24, 79 pp.

POPE, CLIFFORD H., 1937. *Snakes alive and how they live.* Viking Press. 19 East 48th St., New York. 238 pp.

—1955. *The reptile world.* Alfred A. Knopf, 501 Madison Ave., New York 10022, N.Y. xxv, 325, xiii pp., ill.

—1957. *Reptiles round the world.* Knopf, N.Y. 194 pp. (Lower high school level.)

—1961. *The giant snakes.* Alfred Knopf, New York. xviii, 290, vii pp., ill.

PORTER, KENNETH R., 1972. *Herpetology.* W.B. Saunders, Philadelphia. xi, 524 pp., ill. (one of the formal textbooks of herpetology as a discipline; see also Goin and Goin.)

ROBERTS, MERVIN F., 1957. *Snakes.* T.F.H. Publications, Inc., P.O. Box 27, Neptune, N.J. 07753. 34 pp., ill.

—1961. *Beginning the Terrarium.* T.F.H. Publications, Inc., P.O. Box 27, Neptune, N.J. 07753. 32 pp., ill.

—1963. *Your Terrarium.* T.F.H. Publications, Inc., P.O. Box 27, Neptune, N.J. 07753. 64 pp., ill. (color).

—1975. *All about boas and other snakes.* T.F.H. Publications, Inc., P.O. Box 27, Neptune, N.J. 07753. 96 pp., ill. (color).

ROMPELL, SHAY, 1962. "Let's Call it 'Hand' Feeding!", 1962. Bull. Philadelphia Herpetological Soc., 10 (1): 9, 13.

ROTHMAN, NORMA, 1958. "Causes of Death in snakes—and Some Suggested Treatments for Diseases." Bull. Philadelphia Herpetological Soc., 6 (6): 9-12.

—1962. "Miscellaneous Notes on Dri-die and Tedion and Insect Culture." Bull. Philadelphia Herpetological Soc., 10 (1): 25 (see also correction same journal, 1; (2-3): 20).

SCHMIDT, KARL P., and D. DWIGHT DAVIS, 1941. *Field book of snakes of the United States and Canada.* G.P. Putnam's Sons, New York. 365 pp.

SCHMIDT, KARL P., and ROBERT F. INGER, 1957. *Living reptiles of the world.* Hanover House, Garden City, N.Y. 287 pp. (Many photos, 145 in color.)

SHAW, CHARLES E. and SHELDON CAMPBELL, 1974. *Snakes of the American West.* Knopf, New York. xii, 330 pp., 72 pls. (color). (Semi-popular and semitechnical identification manual, with comments on habits, habitat, etc.)

SHERMAN, JANE, 1955. *The real book about snakes.* Garden City Books, Garden City, N.Y. 224 pp., ill. (Elementary.)

STANEK, V.J., 1962. *Introducing non-poisonous snakes.* Golden Pleasure Books. Westbrookhouse, Fulham Broadway, London. 80 pp. A book of excellent photographs.

STEBBINS, ROBERT C., 1954. *Amphibians and reptiles of western north America.* McGraw-Hill Book Co., Inc., 330 W. 42nd St., New York 10036 N.Y. 528 pp., ill.

—1966. *A field guide to western reptiles and amphibians.* Houghton Mifflin, Boston. xvi, 370 pp., 39 pls. (mostly color), 39 figs. 290 maps. (The best general identification manual for western North America, although now a bit out-of-date. A new edition in preparation.)

STIDWORTHY, JOHN, 1971. *Snakes of the world.* Gosset & Dunlap, New York. 159 pp., ill. (color). (Medium level.)

SWINGLE, H.S., 1946. *Raising crickets.* Auburn Univ., Auburn, Ala., Leaflet 22: 1-4, ill.

TARSHIS, I. BARRY, 1960. "Control of Snake Mite (*Ophionyssus natricis*), Other Mites, and Certain Insects with the Sorptive Dust, SG 67." Journ. Econ. Ent., 53 (5): 903-908.

—1961. "Cockroaches for Feeding Purposes." Zoonooz. 34 (4, April): 10-15, ill. (Reprinted in Bull. Philadelphia Herpetological Soc., 1961, vol. 9, no. 6, pp. 13-15, ill.)

TRUITT, JOHN O., 1962. *The common diseases of captive reptiles.* Privately printed. 7 pp. (From the author, 808 Almeira, Coral Gables 34, Fla.)

—1973. *Reptile cages you can build, with notes on the care of captive snakes and lizards.* Ralph Curtis, Hollywood, Fla. iii, 6 Opp; ill. (Mostly cage construction details, 3 pp. on care.)

U.S. DEPT. AGRICULTURE (Washington, D.C.), 1962. *Raising of laboratory white mice and rats.* Agricultural Leaflet 253.

WRIGHT, ALBERT H., and ANNA A. WRIGHT, 1957. *Handbook of snakes of the United States and Canada.* Comstock Publ. Co., Ithaca, N.Y. 2 vols., 1105 pp.

WRIGHT, A. GILBERT, 1967. *In the steps of the great american herpetologist Karl Patterson Schmidt - with nature projects you can do.* Evans, New York. 127 pp., ill. (Biography of one of America's most revered herpetologists; ideas and details for study projects.)

WYKES, ALAN, 1961. *Snake man.: the story of C.J.P. Ionides.* Simon Schuster, New York ix, 273 pp., ill. (A biography of a fugitive from civilization who dedicated his life to collecting animals, especially snakes, in the wilds of Africa. See also Lane.)

ZIM, HERBERT S., and HOBART M. SMITH, 1956. *Reptiles and amphibians.* Golden Nature Guide, Golden Press, New York, 160 pp., ill. color. (75 U.S. species of snakes in color.)

ZWEIFEL, RICHARD G., 1961. "Another Method of Incubating Reptile Eggs." Copeia, 1961 (1): 112-113.

Index

Page numbers set in **bold** type denote illustrations.

T

V

W

Y